M FOR MOU

Born in 1954, Stephen Venables' interest i
school days, when he remembers passin
climbers, George Mallory and Wilfrid Noyce, on his way to music lessons. In 1963 he made his first skiing trip to the Alps (and has been back every year since), and a week's climbing at Fontainebleau in 1970 confirmed his suspicions that 'climbing was an eminently sensible thing to do'!

Now one of Britain's leading mountaineers, Stephen has climbed extensively throughout Europe, the Himalayan and Karakoram ranges, Africa and South America. In 1988, with a four-man team, he climbed a new route up Everest, becoming the first Briton to reach the summit without the aid of supplementary oxygen.

When he is not climbing mountains he lives in Bath with his wife and two sons. He earns his living from lecturing and writing, his previous books being PAINTED MOUNTAINS (which won the Boardman Tasker Prize for the best mountaineering book of 1986), EVEREST, KANGSHUNG FACE and ISLAND AT THE EDGE OF THE WORLD – the story of his expedition to South Georgia.

Other titles in this series

A for Antarctica and
I for Invention by Meredith Hooper

New titles in the series

D for Dolphins by Sarita Kendall
T for Treasurehunting by Ekkehard Schirmer and Olga Norris

Series editor: Meredith Hooper

M *for* MOUNTAINS

Facts and Stories from the Summits of the World

Stephen Venables

Illustrated by

Sally Townsend

A Piccolo Original
PAN MACMILLAN
CHILDREN'S BOOKS

First published 1993 by Pan Macmillan Children's Books
a division of Pan Macmillan Publishers Limited
Cavaye Place London SW10 9PG
and Basingstoke

Associated companies throughout the world

ISBN 0-330-32899-9

1 3 5 7 9 8 6 4 2

A CIP catalogue record for this book is available from the British Library

Phototypeset by Intype, London
Printed and bound in Great Britain
by Cox & Wyman Ltd, Reading, Berkshire

INTRODUCTION

I was eight when I saw my first mountain. I was on holiday with my family. It was a summer evening and, after a long drive from the crowded streets of London, we reached Snowdonia in north Wales. Staring up into the twilight I gazed at gigantic mossy boulders, huge soaring ridges, knarled holly trees clinging to the sides of dark cliffs and, far above the road, mountain summits that seemed impossibly high in the sky. The Welsh mountains had a feeling of wild mystery unlike anything I had experienced before.

The following winter I was taken skiing in the Swiss Alps. These mountains were even grander, with vast shimmering snow-fields, razor-sharp summits and turquoise rivers of ice – my first glaciers. The more I saw of the mountains, the more I was fascinated. Later I learned how to use a climbing rope and ice axe, how to travel safely on the glaciers, and how to climb the snow ridges and rock precipices, finally reaching the magical Alpine summits. I started to organize expeditions further afield, to the Andes of South America, the weird mountains of Africa and to the greatest mountain range of all, in the heart of Asia – the Himalaya.

What exactly is a mountain? The *Concise Oxford English Dictionary* defines a mountain as a 'large natural elevation of the Earth's surface, large or high and steep hill, especially one over 1,000 feet high'. No one can say exactly when a hill becomes a mountain, but when I first saw those mountains of Snowdonia, they were quite different from the gentle, rolling hills where I lived in the south of England.

Mountains are the bumps and wrinkles on the thin skin of the earth. Many of the world's famous mountains, like Kilimanjaro, are volcanoes – gigantic cinder cones, created by molten rock blasting through the earth's crust.

The other main cause of mountains is 'folding' when two land masses press against each other, folding up the earth's crust. The greatest range of all – the Himalaya – was created this way about 50 million years ago when the Indian subcontinent rammed up against Tibet. On the earth's timescale, 50 million years is a very short time. The Himalaya are young mountains, like the European Alps, still being shaped by wind, rain, ice and the grinding action of landslides. By contrast, the smaller mountains of Scotland are much older. They have been worn down to just 1000 metres above sea level, but once they were higher than the Alps are now.

Life has always been hard for people who live in the mountains. Farming is difficult on the steep slopes. The soil is often thin. The weather is frequently stormy and the winters are bitterly cold. The higher you climb above sea level the lower the air temperature drops. Above a certain height there is permanent snow. In the European Alps the snow-line is at about 3,500 metres. In the Himalaya, closer to the heat of the Equator, it is at about 5,000 metres.

It is not just the temperature that drops. There is also a drop in air pressure as you climb higher in the earth's atmosphere, making it harder to get enough oxygen into your lungs. People do live at about 4,000 metres in the Andes and the Himalaya, but above 5,000 metres no human can survive for more than a few months. At 8,000 metres the human body can only survive for a few days, and reaching the summit of Everest, 8,848 metres above sea level, without extra oxygen supplies, is at the limit of human capability.

Mountains are high-altitude deserts – a true wilderness – beautiful, but remote and frightening. For centuries people respected mountains. In many parts of the world they actually worshipped the mountains, treating them as holy places. It was only recently – about 200 years ago – that people began to think of deliberately climbing them. Mont Blanc, Europe's highest mountain, was first climbed in 1786. Everest, far away on the frontier of Tibet and Nepal, was not attempted until 1921 and was only climbed, after many attempts, in 1953.

'Mountaineer' used to mean a person living in the mountains, usually a farmer, shepherd, forester or hunter, who would only climb high above the snow-line if he had to, perhaps to cross a pass to the next valley. Now 'mountaineer' means a person who climbs mountains for sport and adventure.

No one has ever given a simple answer to the question, 'Why climb mountains?' because there is no single answer. I find the mountains beautiful. I love the constantly changing light on the different forms of mountains, like giant natural towers, domes and steeples. I like the excitement of travelling to new places, far from any city. I enjoy the journey up a remote valley, passing through changing zones of forest and flowers, until all vegetation dies out, and we reach a strange world of pure rock, snow and ice. I like the peace and solitude. I enjoy the thrill of gymnastic movement up a steep cliff and the satisfaction of puzzling out difficult moves.

I hate getting up early in the morning, but in the mountains it is always worth it, to be awake at that magical moment when the sun rises. At times climbing is just hard drudgery. There are moments when I feel cold and miserable, shivering on some tiny ledge, wondering if I am ever going to get off the mountain alive. But most things that are worth doing involve some hard work and some uncertainty. In mountaineering the satisfaction comes from controlling the risk and keeping danger to a minimum.

People often ask how one starts mountaineering. In Britain most mountaineers start by rock climbing on some of the smaller cliffs. Then perhaps they do some winter climbing in Scotland, learning to climb on snow and ice. After that they may move on to the Alps, where the climbs are bigger and there is the extra problem of moving on glaciers.

The world's first mountaineering club, the Alpine Club, was founded in London in 1857 and is based in London. Now there are thousands of mountaineering organizations around the world and in many areas there are professional guides and instructors who teach people to climb. In Britain the best guides belong to the Association of British Mountain Guides. To join the association, applicants have to pass very strict tests in rock climbing, Scottish ice climbing, Alpine climbing, First Aid and Rescue.

Anyone can be taught the basics of mountaineering by a professional. Some people who can afford it always climb with guides. However, for mountaineers the real satisfaction comes from taking responsibility for one's own safety, making one's own decisions, whether it is skiing across an untracked glacier, choosing a campsite high on an unclimbed Himalayan peak, or climbing a precipice of granite.

Mountains are dangerous and mountaineers must always be aware of that danger. However, many people enjoy mountains without having to go near their summits. Most ski-runs are extremely safe. Walkers can enjoy the wonderful scenery without having to risk their lives. Botanists can search for rare mountain plants without having to step on snow and ice; geologists can study the bare bones of the earth. Mountains have something to offer nearly everyone and for most of us, who live in crowded cities, they are a wonderful escape. Like the earth's great oceans, deserts and jungles, mountains are a reminder that mankind has only been around for a very short time.

NB

An asterisk* has been put against anything which has an entry of its own elsewhere in the book.

All items of mountaineering equipment have been put under EQUIPMENT.

Acknowledgements

The author and the publisher wish to thank
the following for their permission to
reproduce their photographs:

Robert Anderson: the glacier table.

Anthony Constable-Maxwell: Adams Peak, Ayers Rock, Machhapuchhare and Mount Fuji.

Paul Fatti: the author on Table Mountain.

Oliver Gibbs: Annapurna, Chamonix Aiguilles, the houses in Dzong, the Sherpa and the Tibetan lady.

Karakoram Experience: K2.

The Royal Geographical Society, London: Hillary and Tenzing at 27,000 feet on Everest (page 68).

Beth Wald: Catherine Destivelle.

Ed Webster: inside a crevasse on Everest.

All the remaining photographs are reproduced courtesy of the author.

Scandinavian Mountains
Ural Mountains
Ben Nevis
Mt. Snowdon
Alps
Carparthians
Altai Range
Mt. Blanc
Karakoram
K2
Pyrenees
Mt. Fuji
Everest
Atlas
Mountains
Hindu Kush
Himalaya
AFRICA
PAPUA
NEW GUINEA
Punjak Jaya
Mt. Stanley
Mt. Kenya
Kilimanjaro
Ayers Rock
AUSTRALIA
Table Mountain
Southern

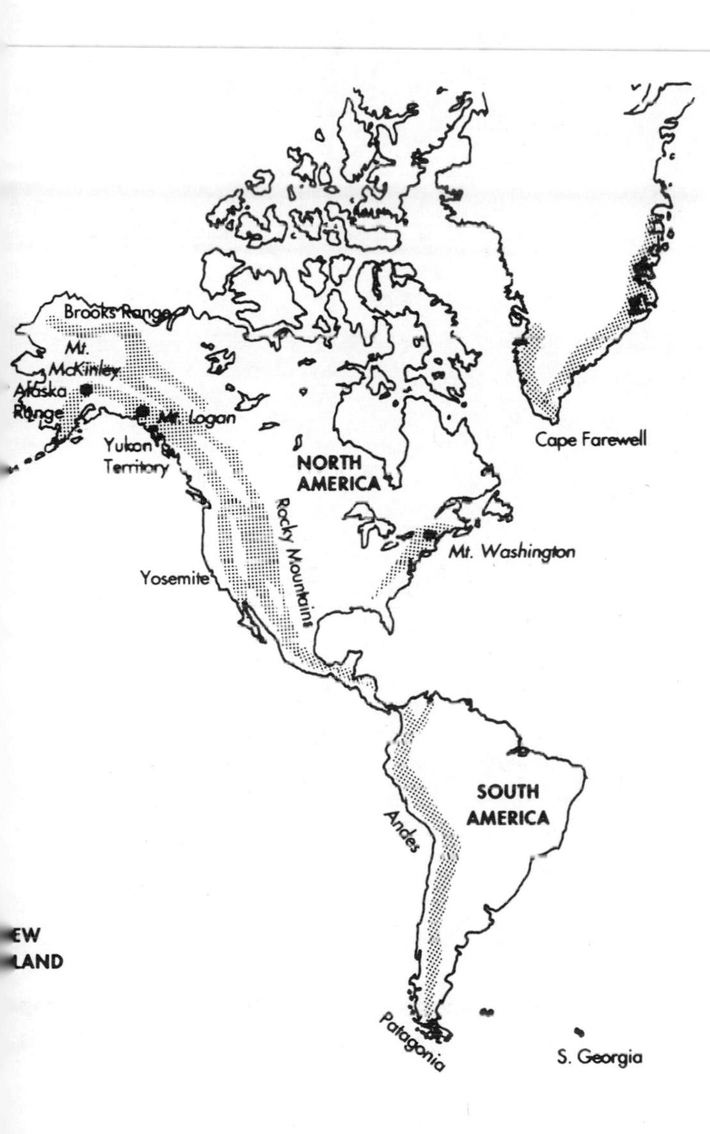
Brooks Range
Mt.
McKinley
Alaska
Range
Mt. Logan
Yukon
Territory
NORTH
AMERICA
Rocky Mountains
Yosemite
Mt. Washington
Cape Farewell
SOUTH
AMERICA
Andes
Patagonia
S. Georgia

EW
LAND

ABSEIL

'Once you reach the summit, how do you get back down again?' is a question mountaineers are frequently asked. Whenever possible they climb down by an easy route, but on very steep slopes it becomes necessary to abseil, a German word meaning down (*ab*) rope (*seil*). The rope is secured to a safe anchor – perhaps a nylon loop round a spike of rock or a metal wedge fixed in a crack – and they take turns to slide down the rope, using special friction brakes clipped into their harnesses.

Usually a double rope is used. When everyone is safely down the rope is pulled through, so that it can be used again. However, the anchor has to be left behind.

Abseiling can be exciting, but it is also dangerous because the mountaineer's life depends on the safety of the anchor and the friction brake. On a long tiring descent it is easy to make mistakes and many experienced mountaineers have been killed when abseiling, or 'rappelling' as it is called in America.

ACONCAGUA

Aconcagua is the highest mountain in South America. The summit is 6960 metres above sea level and lies in Argentina, close to the border with Chile.

ALPENHORN

Farmers and shepherds on the high Swiss Alps sometimes play an extraordinary musical instrument. The alpenhorn is over 2 metres long and so heavy that the bell end has to rest on the ground. It makes a weird low rumbling sound that echoes round the mountains. Thousands of miles away, in the Himalaya, Buddhist monks play similar giant horns in their religious ceremonies.

ALPINE FLOWERS

In summer the Alpine pastures look like brilliant coloured tapestries. Deep blue gentians, purple and yellow primulas, gleaming grey-white Edelweiss* and pink cushions of saxifrage are some of the favourite flowers that survive up to 3000 metres above sea level. Many gardeners grow their own alpine flowers in rockeries, trying to imitate the conditions in the wild. Alpine flowers like rocky soil where the water drains quickly away. They love the summer sunshine, but each winter the leaves and flowers die away, leaving just the roots buried for months under the winter snow.

ALPS

The Alps are the high peaks that stretch in a great arc above the Mediterranean, like a wall dividing Italy in the south from France, Switzerland and Austria in the north. For centuries the Alps were an awesome barrier. The high passes* could only be crossed in summer and even then they were difficult and dangerous. The peasant farmers in the high Alpine valleys lived in isolation, terrified of the high peaks where wicked demons were thought to live.

Now it is all very different. Roads and railways criss-cross the mountains, many of them in long tunnels. Cable cars whisk skiers, walkers and climbers up to the high peaks. Hotels, campsites and mountain huts are crowded with tourists, who come from all over the world to ski, climb or just look at famous mountains like Mont Blanc,* the Matterhorn,* the Eiger* and Monte Rosa.

Leslie Stephen, a famous mountaineer, once described the Alps as 'the Playground of Europe' in his book of the same title published in 1871. More people come each year to play but the mountains are now so crowded and overbuilt that many people are saying, 'Enough! No more hotels, no more ski lifts, no more roads to pollute the Alpine air.' A few farmers remain in the villages. They remember that the word 'alp' originally described the peaceful high pastures where they took their goats and cattle each summer.

ALTITUDE SICKNESS

The air we breathe contains a vital gas: oxygen. Without oxygen, we die. At sea level there is plenty of oxygen, but as we climb to higher altitudes the air pressure gets lower, so it becomes harder to breathe enough air into our lungs to keep our blood supplied with life-giving oxygen: it is 'thin air'. If we were to fly suddenly in a helicopter to the top of Mont Blanc and get out at the summit, which is 4807 metres above sea level, we would feel very sick and dizzy with a splitting headache: here the air pressure is about half what it is at sea level. If the helicopter could land us on top of Everest (8874 metres), most of us would probably faint within minutes and soon die. On the summit of Everest, the air pressure is less than a third of what it is at sea level.

The human body is not designed to live at very high altitudes. Many people begin to feel altitude sickness at 3000 metres. One of the causes is dehydration: the higher you climb out of the earth's atmosphere the drier the air becomes. Even people on skiing holidays at about 2500 metres get very thirsty. On the Himalayan giants between 7000 and 8874 metres high (see DEATH ZONE) it becomes a real problem for mountaineers. Panting from the exertion of climbing in the cold dry air leaves them dried out, dehydrated. Mountaineers must drink as much liquid as possible on a big climb, and because there is no running water at high altitude they carry stoves to melt snow and ice.

Altitude sickness can become very serious. In the Himalaya climbers and trekkers are occasionally paralysed by strokes. In its worst form, altitude sickness causes body fluid to build up in the lungs or the brain. The result is often a quick death.

There is only one reliable cure for altitude sickness – to descend immediately to a safer altitude, where the air pressure is greater. This can be done artificially in a Gamow bag, which is like a sealed plastic sleeping bag. The patient is zipped up inside then the bag is pumped up to the required pressure.

The Gamow bag has saved several lives in the Himalaya. However, it is best to try to avoid becoming ill in the first place. This is done by climbing very slowly, giving the body time to make complicated chemical changes, like building up more red blood cells to extract more oxygen from the lungs. This slow process is called acclimatizing. It usually takes mountaineers at least six weeks to acclimatize for the highest peaks, but descent is never a problem – every step we take down we feel stronger.

ANDES

The Andes is the longest range of mountains on earth. It is like the spine of a skeleton. The skeleton is South America and the Andes form the curving spine, 8000 kilometres long, down the west side of the continent. On one side is the Pacific ocean and on the other, to the east, lie the steamy tropical jungles of the Amazon and Parana rivers.

The Andes start in Colombia and Venezuela. Further south, in Ecuador, there are famous snow-covered volcanoes, like Chimborazo and Cotopaxi. Then come some of the most spectacular mountains of all, in Peru. The highest mountain in Peru is Huascaran, 6768 metres above sea level. Its melting snows feed the river Amazon. The knobbly spine of the continent now curves down to Bolivia. Here, on the Peru–Bolivia border, lies Lake Titicaca, the highest large lake in the world, famous for its fishing boats made from reeds. Just south of Titicaca is La Paz, the capital city of Bolivia, nearly 4000 metres above sea level.

The final 3500 kilometres of the Andes range marks the long frontier between Chile and Argentina. The mountains march right down to the island of Tierra del Fuego and the stormy tip of South America, Cape Horn. There the Andes end, but not completely, for even further south they emerge again from the sea. These mountains on the Antarctic peninsula are not called the Andes, but geologists say that they are part of the same mountain range.

ANNAPURNA

Only fourteen mountains in the world are higher than 8000 metres above sea level. Annapurna, in the Himalaya, was the first one to be climbed. It was 1950 and the King of Nepal had only just started to allow foreigners into his country. A French team of top mountaineers had permission to attempt either Annapurna or another 8000-metre peak, Dhauligiri. No mountaineers had ever been near the mountains before and the maps were inaccurate. For the French climbers and their Nepalese porters, the first job was to find a way onto the mountains.

After weeks of exploring they found a possible route up the north side of Annapurna, but by now it was late May and the big summer rains of the monsoon were approaching. The French had to race up the huge mountain in just three weeks. In the nick of time two men reached the summit:* Louis Lachenal and the expedition leader, Maurice Herzog.

The expedition had been successful, but Herzog and Lachenal paid a huge price for their success. A violent storm caught them high on the mountain. With their companions they only just managed to struggle back down through it. They spent a ghastly night out in a crevasse* with only one sleeping bag between four people. They became snow blind.* Their toes and fingers turned black with frostbite.* They only just got down alive and afterwards most of their fingers and toes had to be amputated.

In spite of his terrible injuries Herzog was thrilled with

his triumph on Annapurna. Although he would never again be able to tackle serious climbs, he felt that other different adventures would follow. As he wrote at the end of his book, *Annapurna*: 'There are other Annapurnas in the lives of men.'

ARÊTE

Most of the world's mountains were shaped by erosion.* Over millions of years they have been formed into towers and pyramids, with sharp ridges separating the different faces. These sharp ridges are known by the French word 'arête'. Rock arêtes are often spiked with great towers. A snow arête can be a clean, sharp, white line, but sometimes it is decorated with cornices* and great bulging towers called snow mushrooms.

ATLAS MOUNTAINS

Far in the north of Africa lies a mountain range which suffers both the extreme cold and snowy winters of the north, and the hot, dry summers of the south. Toubkal, at 4165 metres, is the highest peak of the Atlas Mountains, and at its foot the local Berber tribes farm the high valleys.

AVALANCHE

It was the afternoon of 20 January 1951. In the Swiss village of Andermatt everything was quiet. It had been snowing for days. No one had seen anything like it before. The trees and houses were weighed down under immense mounds of snow; the sky was dark and the snow was still falling, piling up deeper and deeper on the steep mountain slope above the village.

On the outskirts of the village stood a large house called the Muhle, divided into flats. That afternoon eight of the tenants – men, women and children – were in the building. Two more, Stephan Theuss and Wilhelm Lutz, were shovelling snow off the roof, chatting as they worked. Suddenly they were interrupted by an extraordinary noise, a mixture of roaring, hissing, humming and whining. The next thing Lutz remembered was seeing a dark, swirling cloud blasting towards him. He rushed to climb back into the house, but just as he was half-way through the window, he felt himself lifted up with the whole roof and flung through the air.

Wilhelm Lutz landed 20 metres away, near one of the village shops. When he looked back towards the Muhle he just saw a huge mound of snow. The house had disappeared completely.

Other villagers rushed to help, digging with shovels into the great mound of snow, but the house had been smashed and crushed under the immense pressure of the avalanche. Now the snow was setting hard like concrete. That afternoon the rescuers found Stephan Theuss. He was dead. It took three days to find the remaining eight people, all dead, crushed under the great weight of compacted snow.

Avalanches have always been a threat to the high Alpine villages, but that terrible weekend in 1951 was the worst in Switzerland's history. Many people in other villages were killed. Now, on the slopes above Andermatt and other villages, steel and concrete fences have been built to stop the snow from sliding. All over the Alps, villages have had to build safety barriers, particularly in areas where too many trees have been cut down – for trees are the best protection of all.

There are many different kinds of avalanche. The giant powder-snow avalanches take off like express trains. Wet avalanches slide like sticky porridge. Sometimes a new layer of snow does not stick properly to old snow and a whole layer, or slab, breaks off with a loud bang. Sometimes a crumbling tower of glacier ice will crash down and start a snow avalanche. Skiers often set off avalanches. To avoid this danger, ski-lift staff sometimes close a popular ski run so that they can fire a mortar into an unstable snow slab. The explosion sets off an avalanche, leaving the slope safe for skiers to enjoy themselves.

Mountaineers and cross-country skiers have to learn about avalanches so that they can avoid danger. The most risky time is just after a big snowfall, but changing winds and temperatures can also make a slope suddenly dangerous. Even the most experienced mountaineers are sometimes caught out, particularly in the Himalaya.* In 1991 an entire expedition of seventeen Chinese and Japanese climbers disappeared in a huge avalanche.

Avalanches are terrifying but victims sometimes survive. If you are caught by one you must fight hard, with swimming movements, to stay on top of the snow. You must also keep your mouth firmly shut to avoid swallowing snow dust. If the worst comes to the worst and you are buried, hold your arms in front of your face, keeping a space of air to breathe.

AYERS ROCK

The highest mountain in Australia is Mount Kosciusko (2134 metres), but the most beautiful and extraordinary is Ayers Rock, the largest isolated monolith in the world. It is a gigantic hump of bare sandstone, lying in the desert like a strange prehistoric animal. In the evening it glows deep red in the light of the setting sun. This beautiful mountain is one of the most popular tourist attractions in Australia, but for the Aborigines who have lived here for thousands of years, Ayers Rock is a sacred place called Uluru. To them Uluru is the source of the power of creation.

BALLOONING

In 1978 Reinhold Messner* and Peter Habeler became the first people to reach the summit of Everest* (8874 metres) without bottled oxygen. However, 116 years earlier two

Englishmen went much higher without oxygen – in a hot air balloon.

James Glaisher and Henry Coxwell took off from Wolverhampton on 5 September 1862. The balloon rose quickly into the air. Glaisher read the altitude on the barometer, as the balloon climbed to 6000 metres, 7000 metres then 8000 metres. By now the two men were bitterly cold and could barely breathe in the thin air.* As the balloon approached 9000 metres Glaisher's arms and legs began to feel heavy. Then he lost his sight and quickly fainted. The balloon was still rising, but luckily Coxwell was still just conscious. He had to pull open a valve to make the balloon descend but, like Glaisher, his arms felt limp and useless. In a last desperate effort he managed to reach up with his neck and grab the cord in his teeth, pulling the valve open.

The balloon started to descend immediately and Glaisher soon came round. By checking the time on his watch he calculated how high the balloon had climbed while he was unconscious. According to his calculations, the balloon had reached about 10,500 metres before Coxwell pulled the valve cord and saved the two men's lives.

Nowadays no one would dream of flying so high without breathing equipment. Nevertheless, balloons are still very difficult to control, because they are at the mercy of the winds. This is particularly true near mountains, where air currents are difficult to predict. However, in fine weather, ballooning is a wonderful way to see the mountains.

One of the great ballooning challenges was to fly over the summit of Everest.* This was finally achieved in 1991 by a team from Britain and Australia. First a huge team of porters had to carry the enormous balloons, the baskets, burners, fuel cylinders, food, camera equipment, weather satellite gear and a hundred other things to the base camp at Gokyo, on the Nepalese side of Everest. Gokyo is 4750 metres above sea level. From there, Leo Dickinson and Chris Dewhirst took off in the first balloon, followed by Eric Jones and Andy Elson in the second. Unlike Glaisher and Coxwell, they were dressed in warm down clothing and they breathed from oxygen cylinders. Each man also wore a parachute on his back, in case he had to jump out in an emergency.

Despite all this modern equipment it was a risky flight. The balloons had to climb fast, burning fuel rapidly, to make sure they cleared the top of the mountain. Once they reached 9000 metres they were in the jet-stream winds,* zooming across the top of the world at 100 kph. Jones and Elson had some frightening moments. To achieve maximum lift, their burner was so hot that the wires holding the basket to the balloon started to snap. The balloon also looked as though it was going to be blown into the side of the mountain.

Meanwhile the other balloon had flown right over the summit of Everest and was now 75 kilometres to the east, over Tibet, and running out of fuel. The pilot, Dewhirst, had to make a rushed landing. As the balloon came down towards the ground it was caught by a gust of wind and smashed into a rock. Then it took off again before coming down a second time, flinging Dickinson and Dewhirst to the ground. Dickinson was badly injured and all his cameras were smashed, but he was relieved to discover that the films inside the cameras were undamaged. Once they were developed, he had a unique collection of photographs and a television film, showing the balloons flying right over the summit of Everest.

BEN NEVIS

Ben is the Gaelic word for hill or mountain and Ben Nevis is the highest mountain in the British Isles. The summit is 1344 metres above sea level. That is not very high compared to other mountains around the world. However, Ben Nevis rises straight from the seashore, so it seems quite big when you look up from the town of Fort William. The south side is a great rounded hump but on the north side are steep cliffs 600 metres high. These cliffs are popular with rock climbers* and in winter they often give good ice climbing.

BIGO BOG

If you have walked far in the mountains of Scotland or Ireland you will know what bogs are like: spongy mosses, reeds and cotton grass growing in thick oozy mud. One of the finest bogs of all is in Africa. It is called Bigo Bog and it covers about 4 square kilometres, filling a high valley in the Ruwenzori mountains, on the western border of Uganda. The bog is surrounded by extraordinary plants called giant groundsels and giant lobelias, which look as though they come from a land of dinosaurs. There is also a forest of giant heathers, which grow up to 15 metres high. The atmosphere of the Ruwenzori mountains is so mysterious that they are known as the 'Mountains of the Moon'.

Sir Henry Stanley was the first European to see the Ruwenzori mountains, in 1876. His discovery proved correct the rumours of snowy mountains at the heart of Africa. As early as AD 150, the Roman geographer, Claudius Ptolemy, had written about 'the Mountain of the Moon, whose snows feed the lakes, sources of the Nile'.

BIVOUAC

A big mountain climb often lasts several days. If we do not want to carry tents, we often 'bivouac' – camp out – in the open. Usually we each have a sleeping bag and an insulated foam mat to keep warm, and perhaps a windproof 'bivouac sack' to pull over the sleeping bag. Cooking is done on a small gas or petrol stove and often we have to melt snow to make water for drinks and meals.

The important thing on a bivouac is to get as comfortable as possible. Sometimes there is a natural ledge. At other times we build a platform out of rocks. Sometimes it is easier to dig a ledge, or even a cave, in the snow. However, there are times when we have to make do with the tiniest ledges, sitting upright all night and getting very little sleep.

If the bivouac is perched above a big drop, it is vital to stay tied to the mountain all night, in case we roll over in our sleep. On very steep climbs with no ledges at all, we bivouac in hammocks or carry up collapsible platforms, called Portaledges.*

Sometimes climbers are caught unprepared and have to bivouac without even a sleeping bag. In 1953 the Austrian climber Hermann Buhl* had to bivouac above 8000 metres, near the summit of Nanga Parbat. In 1975 the British climbers Doug Scott and Dougal Haston had to bivouac even higher without sleeping bags, at 8750 metres, very close to the summit of Everest.* They didn't get much sleep, but they survived!

BLANK ON THE MAP

> A fascinating way of spending a few hours of leisure is to sit down with a paper and pencil and work out in minute detail the preparation for an expedition into unexplored country. The fact that there is very little chance of carrying out the project matters little. These dream expeditions can be staged in any corner of the world. I have imagined them in the forbidden mountains of Nepal, and in the wind-swept ice peaks of Tierra del Fuego, and across the antarctic continent.

Eric Shipton wrote those words in 1937, as the introduction to his book *Blank on the Map*. In those days, before satellites could photograph the earth from space, there were still unknown areas left blank on the map. In 1937 Shipton led an expedition to explore one of these blanks – a great wilderness of peaks and glaciers in the Karakoram range. Before starting that expedition he had already become one of the world's most successful mountain explorers. He had climbed high on the north side of Everest*; with Bill Tilman he had discovered the route to the Indian peak of Nanda Devi;* and in Africa he had made the second ascent of Mount Kenya.

Shipton was always dreaming about new mountain adventures, but what made him different from so many dreamers was that his dreams usually came true. In 1950 when the mountains of Nepal were opened up for the first time to foreigners it was Shipton who led some of the first explorations. Later he *did* visit the ice-swept peaks of Tierra del Fuego, at the tip of South America. Right up to his death in 1976 he continued to explore remote mountain country around the world.

Today many mountaineers are still inspired by Shipton's example. He always travelled with the minimum of fuss and bother, keeping luggage to an absolute minimum. That way he and his companions were free to cover huge distances, always keen to see what lay round the corner or over the next pass. Shipton loved this life of discovery and adventure. In another of his books, *That Untravelled World*, he wrote: 'There are few treasures of more lasting worth than the experiences of a way of life that is in itself wholly satisfying. Such, after all, are the only possessions of which no fate, no cosmic catastrophe can deprive us; nothing can alter the fact if for one moment in eternity we have really lived.'

WALTER BONATTI

A butterfly landed on the snow, fluttered its wings feebly, collapsed and died. Walter Bonatti watched with tears in his eyes. He felt a special sympathy for the butterfly that had flown so high, only to perish in the cold mountain air. Tomorrow he, too, might die. But there was no turning back now. He had to go up, alone, on the mountain.

It was 1955. The previous year the Italian mountaineer Walter Bonatti had been in Pakistan climbing the world's second highest mountain, K2.* He had worked hard for the team, but he had not been chosen to go to the summit. He had returned bitterly disappointed to his home in the Alps.

Now, a year later, he was determined to make his mark with a fantastic difficult new climb. For years he had been studying the Dru, a huge steeple of rock in the Mont Blanc* range, soaring 1000 metres into the sky. No one had ever climbed its smooth vertical south-west pillar. Bonatti was determined to climb the pillar. Alone.

For six nights Bonatti slept on the pillar, tied to minute ledges. By day he climbed, metre by metre, up the wall of smooth granite. It was almost like engineering – hammering steel pegs and wooden wedges into cracks in the rock, protecting himself with his long nylon rope. Bonatti's only companion was the huge rucksack full of supplies which he hauled up after himself. On the second day he accidentally smashed his finger with the hammer. On the third day he ran out of water. Paraffin from the stove spilt in his food. He was tormented by hunger, thirst and agonizing cramps in his arms.

The most frightening moment came on the fifth day. Bonatti had reached a dead end. The rock was completely smooth with not even a tiny crack to make progress. There was no chance of retreating; he had to find a way up. Then he noticed a huge block sticking out of the wall 10 metres to his right. It was his only chance.

He tied all the pegs and wedges on one end of the rope to make an anchor. Then he flung the rope across the gap, lassoing the block with his anchor. Now came the awful moment of truth. The rope stretched sideways to the distant anchor. Below him, the wall dropped giddily. If the anchor failed he would hurtle 1000 metres through the air.

He grasped the rope, looked one more time at the anchor, then swung in a wild dizzy fall through space. The rope jerked. Bonatti swung back left then came to a halt, safe below the anchor. It had held. Now he just had to pull himself up the rope and continue up the new line of holds.

Bonatti arrived safely on the summit the next day. His new climb up the Dru was a remarkable achievement and to this day his route is called the Bonatti Pillar.

In 1958 Bonatti returned to Pakistan. K2 had now been climbed but Bonatti made the first ascent of another difficult mountain, Gasherbrum IV, which is almost 8000 metres above sea level.

In 1965 Bonatti decided to retire from serious mountaineering but first he made one farewell climb, a difficult new route up the North Wall of the Matterhorn.* He climbed it alone in the middle of winter. As on the Dru climb, Bonatti's companion was his rucksack. However, this time he also took a teddy bear for company during

the long, bitterly cold winter nights. On the sixth day, when he reached the summit, aeroplanes circled in the sky, saluting one of the greatest mountaineers of all time.

BONG see CLIMBING GEAR

CHRIS BONINGTON

Mountaineers love to be first up a particular route or mountain. One person who has collected more firsts than almost anyone else is the British mountaineer Chris Bonington. He was in the first team to climb the Old Man of Hoy, an amazing rock tower that rises out of the sea off the Orkney islands. He was in the first British team to climb the famous North Face of the Eiger.* In 1970 he led the first ascent of the South Face of Annapurna,* one of the hardest climbs that had ever been done in the Himalaya" at that time. In 1975 he organized the first ascent of the difficult South-West Face of Everest.* In 1985 he himself went to the summit of Everest by another route. He was fifty and the oldest person to have climbed to the top of the world, but nine days later a fifty-five-year-old American, Dick Bass, reached the summit.

Chris Bonington was thrilled to reach the summit of Everest in 1985 but that was not the end of his climbing. He continued to climb almost every day while at home in the English Lake District and to go on expeditions to remote parts of the world at least once every year.

BRIDGES

Building paths and roads through mountain country is always a complicated business. One of the problems is getting across all the deep river valleys and gorges. Bridges, of course, are the answer. They are often beautiful structures. In Switzerland, the mountain roads and railways are famous for their elegant bridges. The early ones were built of stone with curved arches, but nowadays they are constructed from giant sections of steel and concrete.

In many parts of the Himalaya there are no roads, but the footpaths have some amazing bridges. Often they are suspension bridges, hanging across huge gorges. Some of the oldest ones are made from bamboo or cables of twisted twigs, swaying high above the roaring torrent.

HERMANN BUHL

The Austrian mountaineer Hermann Buhl tiptoed along a narrow ledge. Beneath his feet the mountain fell in a single terrifying drop, 4000 metres to the valley. His height above sea level was 8000 metres. He was in the 'death zone'.* His throat was parched dry from panting in the thin dry air. His legs were shaky with exhaustion. Since he left his tent at two thirty that morning of 3 July 1953, he had climbed up 1200 metres and had covered a horizontal distance of 4 kilometres. No one had ever before climbed so far in one day at that altitude. Now it was six o'clock in the evening and Buhl had almost reached the summit of Nanga Parbat in Pakistan.

At the end of the ledge there was a steep crack in the rock, leading upwards, which Buhl managed to climb, but it was so exhausting that he collapsed at the top and had to crawl on hands and knees up the final snow slope. At seven he reached the summit. The sun was setting and Hermann Buhl was completely alone on top of the seventh highest mountain in the world. No person had ever trodden there before.

It was a wonderful victory, but the lonely climber knew that he would never get back to the tent that night. To make matters worse, it had been blazing hot all day and Buhl had left all his warm clothes in his rucksack a long way back, when he took them off in the morning. Now the temperature was dropping way below freezing. Buhl had

on just two thin layers of clothing and there was no chance of getting back to his rucksack that day. He began his descent, but soon the ridge became too difficult to climb in the dark. There was not even a ledge big enough for him to sit down, so he had to spend the night standing up, leaning against a rock. At 8000 metres it was bitterly cold.

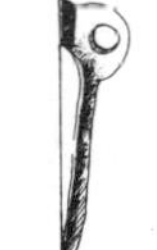

It was a torture that most people could not have survived. But Buhl did survive. At first light in the morning he continued down the ridge. It took the rest of that day to get back to the tent where his companions were waiting. When Buhl arrived he was too weak to speak. His toes were dead from frostbite,* after the terrible night in the open, and his face was unrecognizable. He was only twenty-nine but now, after his struggle to the summit of Nanga Parbat, he looked like an old man.

Hermann Buhl recovered from his extraordinary adventure. Four years later he returned to Pakistan to climb another of the great 8000-metre peaks, Broad Peak. Then, trying another mountain with his friend Kurt Diemberger, he fell through an overhanging cornice* of snow. He was never seen again.

Just before he died, Buhl wrote a book about all his climbs. He called it *Nanga Parbat Pilgrimage*.

FANNY BULLOCK-WORKMAN

In 1912 only men were allowed to vote in elections in Britain. However, many women were fighting for the right to vote. Fanny Bullock-Workman carried a banner saying 'Votes For Women' to the top of a high mountain pass* in India. With her husband, William Bullock-Workman, she made many long journeys in the Himalaya* and Karakoram mountains, exploring unknown glaciers.* She was a tough woman, rather bossy and unpopular with the local porters who carried all her equipment and supplies.

CHANGABANG

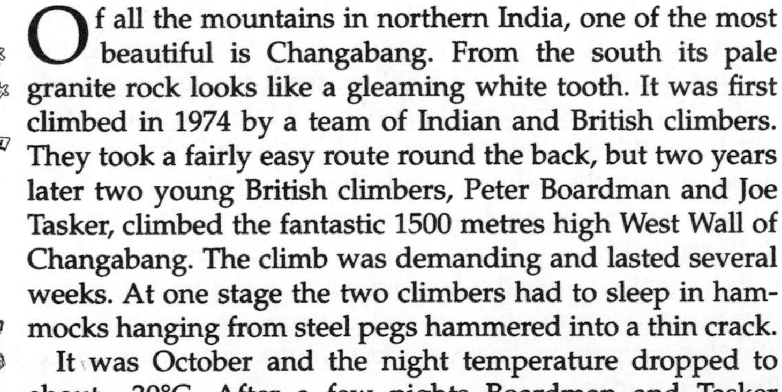

Of all the mountains in northern India, one of the most beautiful is Changabang. From the south its pale granite rock looks like a gleaming white tooth. It was first climbed in 1974 by a team of Indian and British climbers. They took a fairly easy route round the back, but two years later two young British climbers, Peter Boardman and Joe Tasker, climbed the fantastic 1500 metres high West Wall of Changabang. The climb was demanding and lasted several weeks. At one stage the two climbers had to sleep in hammocks hanging from steel pegs hammered into a thin crack.

It was October and the night temperature dropped to about –30°C. After a few nights Boardman and Tasker decided that sleeping in hammocks was too miserable and uncomfortable so they abseiled* back down to their base camp in the valley. When they climbed back up again a few days later they found a snow patch on the side of the cliff, where they cut out a ledge with room for a tiny tent. However, as the outside edge of the tent stuck out over a drop of about 1000 metres, they took turns at sleeping on the outside. From this precarious camp, they worked away at the remaining part of the climb, fixing ropes so that they could climb up and down from the tent each day. Eventually they climbed a deep chimney* capped by a huge booming flake of rock wedged across the chimney and weighing many tonnes. Behind the flake there was a narrow gap which they called the 'keyhole'. Once they had squeezed through the keyhole the worst difficulties were over and two days later they reached the summit of Changabang.

The West Wall of Changabang was one of the most remarkable climbs ever achieved in the Himalaya.* Boardman and Tasker went on to do many other big climbs but sadly they both disappeared in 1982, high on the North-East Ridge of Everest.* Peter Boardman's body was discovered by a Russian climber ten years later, resting in the snow at about 8200 metres, but Joe Tasker's has never been found. Like the story of Mallory and Irvine, who disappeared near the top of Everest in 1924, the loss of Boardman and Tasker remains one of the unsolved mountain mysteries.

CHIMNEY

Most rock climbs follow lines of weakness in the cliff. Often the most obvious line is a thin crack into which you can jam the tips of your fingers. Wider cracks are climbed by hand jamming. When a crack is big enough to get right inside, climbers call it a chimney.

Back and foot technique for climbing a chimney

On the granite cliffs of Yosemite, in California, famous chimneys soar up for hundreds of metres between completely smooth slabs of rock. Narrow chimneys involve a lot of awkward squirming, but when they become a bit wider you can climb more easily, pressing your hands, knees and feet against one wall and your back against the other. If the chimney becomes wider still, you climb by 'bridging', with your arms and feet stretched wide between the walls. Sometimes a chimney is blocked by a 'chockstone' of wedged rock. If you are lucky, there is room to squeeze behind the chockstone. Otherwise you have to pull yourself round the outside.

CLIMBING GEAR

It is possible to climb overhanging cliffs with no gear at all, relying just on the skill in your hands and feet. However, you need very tough feet to manage without special shoes or boots. And unless you can guarantee not to fall off, you need safety equipment like ropes, harness, karabiners, nuts and so on. Then on high mountains you also need special clothing, ice climbing and survival gear. Before a big climb you must check and recheck every detail, deciding exactly what you need to take, and leaving behind anything that is not essential.

Here is a list of the equipment two people might take on a big Himalayan climb:

SHARED GEAR

Climbing

ropes: two 50-metre 9-mm ropes
nylon tape slings: 5
karabiners: 20
rock pitons: 5
nuts: 8
friends: 3
tubular titanium ice screws: 5
snowstakes: 2
jumars: one pair

Bivouac

lightweight dome tent
hanging gas stove with cooking pan
gas cylinders: five 250 ml cylinders
bivouac brush (for brushing snow off clothes and sleeping bag)
snow shovel
plenty of matches
maps, photographs or notes about the route
first aid kit

PERSONAL GEAR

Large rucksack, containing

lightweight foam sleeping mat
down sleeping bag
large plastic mug
spoon
cigarette lighter
spare mittens
dry socks to change into at night
spare films
sun cream
whistle
headtorch (worn on helmet when climbing in the dark)
loo paper

Climbing

helmet
crampons } carried in rucksacks when doing pure rock climbing
ice axe
ice hammer
climbing harness

Clothing

(maximum clothing for the coldest temperatures)
plastic climbing boots with padded inners
gaiters (keep snow out of boots)
windproof jacket with hood
windproof trousers
down filled jacket
(down trousers for the very coldest climbs)
fleece Balaclava hat
windproof mittens with fleece liners
fleece trousers
fleece jacket
thermal underwear
socks

camera
sun glasses

Bong

The bong was invented in the 1960s in California for climbing on the smooth granite cliffs of Yosemite (pronounced Yohsemmitty). Some of the climbs followed wide straight cracks splitting the granite walls. The climbers wedged feet and fists into the cracks to pull themselves up, but they needed something to clip the ropes to, in case they fell off. So they hammered special wide pegs into the cracks. The pegs were made from sheets of steel bent into U-shapes. They made a noise

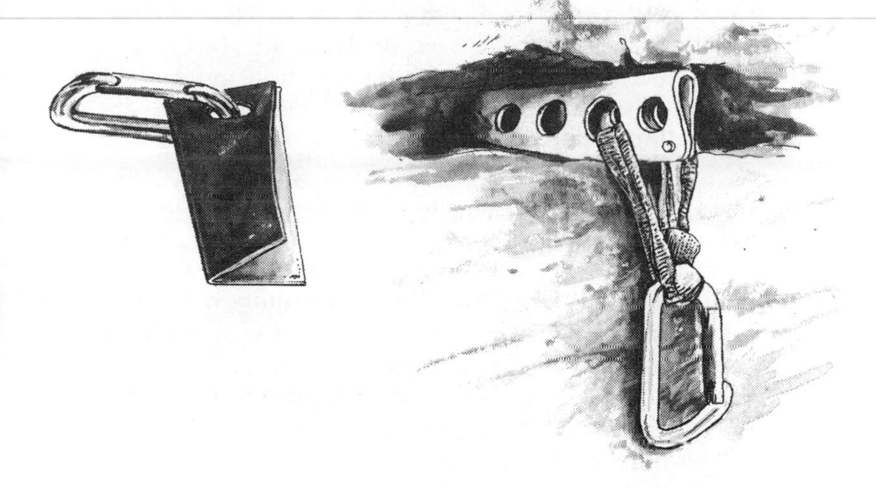

like cowbells as they were hammered in, so they were called 'bongs'.

Climbers still use bongs sometimes, but nowadays we more often use adjustable 'friends' (see page 26), which are easier to put in and take out.

Crampon

Human beings were not designed to climb on steep snow and ice. They need special tools. In the early days of mountaineering, climbers used long ice axes to chop out steps. Nowadays they still carry ice axes, often one in each hand, but they are mainly used as handholds, because on their feet they wear special ice-climbing spikes called crampons. (See the back cover of this book.)

Imagine that you are on a mountain wall, climbing up dry rock. You come to the start of a steep sheet of ice, so you stop on a ledge, take off your rucksack and unpack a pair of crampons. Each crampon is a set of twelve steel spikes on a metal frame. You are probably wearing tough, rigid mountaineering boots, in which case you can attach the crampons with clips, rather like ski bindings. Now each of your feet has twelve sharp steel spikes. Ten of them point down, but the two front ones point forwards, like claws, from the toe of your boot. You are now equipped to climb steep ice.

Of course, it takes a little practice to get used to crampons. You have to walk with your feet well apart, to avoid catching points on your trousers. Then, on steeper snow and ice, you learn to climb sideways, zig-zagging across the slope. After a while it feels quite natural to move around with spikes on your feet, like a specially adapted mountain animal.

On really steep ice, you climb straight up, facing the slope and kicking in the toes of your boots; it is really just the front claws on each boot that hold you to the mountain. Balancing like this, on the claw-tips of your toes, with an ice axe in each hand, it is possible to climb vertical or even overhanging ice. This extreme ice climbing is exhausting. It requires a strong nerve and good technique.

Friend

During the 1960s, the American scientist Ray Jardine helped plan the first spacecraft landings on Mars. Then he stopped working for the North American Space Agency (NASA) and became a climber, spending months at a time living and climbing in California's Yosemite valley. Many of the rock climbs in Yosemite follow vertical or overhanging cracks. Often, the sides of the cracks are smooth and parallel; sometimes they flare outwards, making it hard to place gadgets into which to clip the rope. In the early 1970s, the only gadgets available were removable alloy wedges called nuts, or steel pegs and bongs that had to be hammered in and out of the cracks.

The pegs damaged the granite; the nuts did not need hammering but in many cracks they would not hold

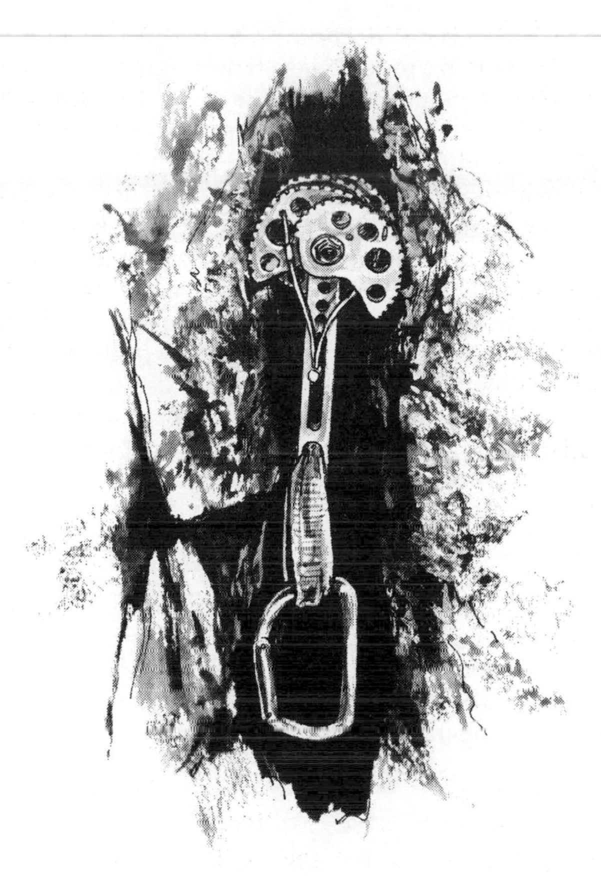

properly. Ray Jardine decided to evolve a completely new protection device that would hold in any crack or hollow, even upside down. It took five years of trial and error to perfect.

The final result was a strange-looking gadget. The picture shows what it looked like. The four curved pieces of alloy are spring-loaded 'cams', attached to a long stem. By pulling on a trigger, you squeeze the cams together and push them into a crack in the rock. When you let go of the trigger the cams push out against the sides of the crack. A loop at the end of the stem is then clipped into your climbing rope. If you fall off, giving a pull on the rope, the stem pulls against the cams. The harder the stem pulls, the harder the cams push out against the crack walls, jamming tighter and tighter.

The great thing about Jardine's device is that it can be placed easily and quickly in almost any crack. It comes in nine sizes, but each size fits quite a wide range of cracks, expanding until it jams securely. The device has helped many a panicking climber on the point of falling off and most people would agree that Ray Jardine chose a good name for his invention when he called it the friend.

Friends are useful for protecting difficult climbs, but like all climbing equipment they are no guarantee of safety unless the owner knows how to use them properly.

Headlamp

One of the worst things about a big snow and ice climb is that you often have to get up in the middle of the night and start climbing in the dark so that you can climb any dangerous sections before the sun comes up and melts the snow, loosening avalanches or falling

rocks. Unless there is a very bright moon you need a torch. As you use both hands to climb, you wear a head-lamp, rather like a miner's, strapped to your helmet. That way it is possible to do even quite difficult climbing in the dark.

Although night climbing can be cold and frightening, it all seems worth it when the dawn arrives and you are enjoying the first precious moments of a new day while the valleys are still sleeping deep in shadow. Later, when the sun blazes down, melting the snow to slush, you feel glad to have done as much climbing as possible during the cool hours of night and early morning.

Ice axe

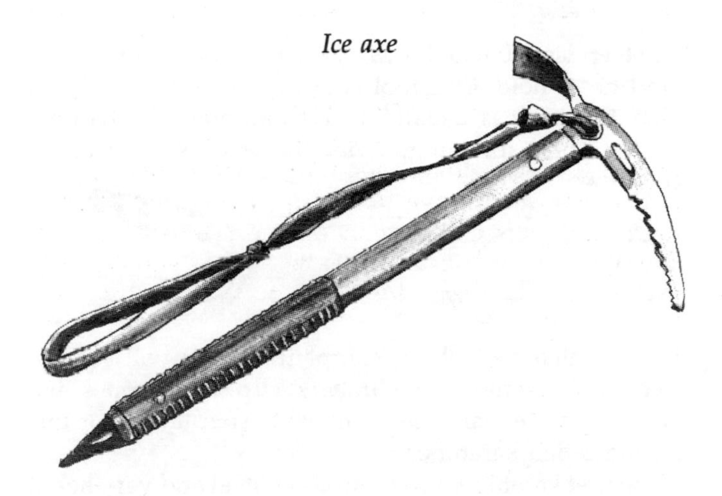

The modern ice axe has a strong metal shaft. At one end there is a spike for plunging into the snow. At the other end is the 'head', set like the top of a T on the end of the shaft. The head has an adze, like an axe, for chopping steps in the ice, and a long thin pick, which is vital on steep ice. The mountaineer whacks it into the ice so that he has something to hold on to.

Ice hammer

On steep ice we usually carry two ice tools so that each hand has a hold. One tool is always an ice axe with an adze; the other is usually an ice hammer. The hammer head is used for banging in pitons (see opposite) or ice screws.

Karabiner

If you watch a climbing competition you will see that every few metres the climbers clip their ropes into anchors on the wall. The removable snaplinks that they use are called karabiners.

The first karabiners were made of steel and very heavy. These days they are made from light alloys – which is just as well because on a big climb you might carry up to forty karabiners.

Karabiners keep you linked to the mountain. You use them to clip into anchors as you lead and then the second person unclips them when he follows. At night you use them to make a bivouac, clipping in tents or hammocks, bits of equipment and, most important of all, yourself.

Nut

During the 1960s British rock climbers were attempting increasingly difficult climbs. Sometimes the only way of protecting the climbers on these rock faces was to wedge a pebble in a crack, thread a loop round the pebble and clip the climbing rope into the loop with a karabiner. The idea was that if the leader fell off, his weight would be held on the pebble.

Then someone had the idea of using steel nuts instead of pebbles, and instead of a pocketful of pebbles, climbers would carry a selection of hexagonal machine nuts, each with its loop of cord threaded through the hole. Soon people had the idea of making nuts specially for climbers, and as well as hexagonal nuts, they made wedge-shaped nuts, which can make even better anchors.

Now alloy nuts come in a great variety of shapes and sizes. The biggest are like great cowbells, on rope loops. The tiniest 'micro nuts' are smaller than a fingernail, and threaded with very thin wire.

Piton

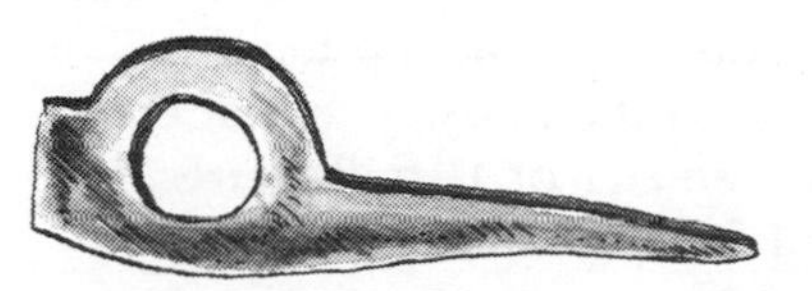

During the 1920s when climbers began to explore steeper rock faces, they invented the piton, a steel peg which can be hammered into a crack in the

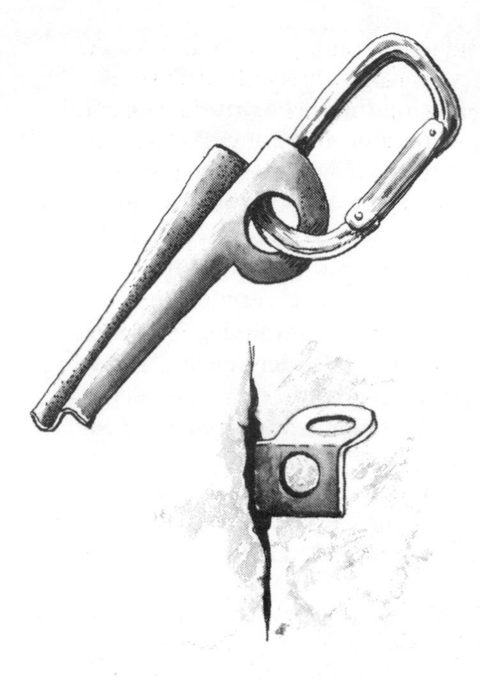

rock to provide a secure anchor. The head of the piton is a round eye, into which a karabiner can be clipped. Pitons come in different shapes and sizes, to fit all kinds of cracks. The largest, called bongs (see page 24), are up to 10 centimetres wide. The tiniest piton, called a rurp (Realized Ultimate Reality Piton!), has a blade not much bigger than a man's fingernail, but if it is used skilfully, hammered into a minute hairline crack, it can support a climber's weight.

Rope

The rope is a mountaineer's life-line. It makes it possible to go where human beings were never meant to go. But the mountaineer has to know how to use the rope wisely: it is not a guarantee of safety.

Climbing ropes used to be made of twisted hemp. They were heavy and stiff, particularly when wet or frozen, and they were not very strong. Nowadays every climber uses a nylon kernmantel rope. The 'kern' is the core, made from many parallel strands of nylon cord. The 'mantel' is the tough woven sheath that holds it all together. Because all the cords run parallel, a kernmantel rope has a lot of stretch. This helps take up the shock of a big fall, limiting damage to the body. A full strength kernmantel rope, with a diameter of 11 millimetres, has a breaking strain of about 2 tonnes.

Ropes do not last for ever, becoming worn and weak. They must be handled with care, especially if there are sharp edges of rock which could cut through the sheath. Even modern ropes can get wet and frozen; they can kink and tie themselves in knots. When mountaineers are fighting through a storm, tired and hungry, they must be patient with their ropes.

Sometimes climbers use thin ropes to save weight, but this is risky. The famous American climber John Harlin was killed during the first ascent of the Eiger Direct, when a 7-millimetre rope broke. Jerzy Kukuczka, at one time one of the best Himalayan climbers in the world, fell 4000 metres to his death when a 6-millimetre rope broke near the summit of Lhotse.

Rucksack

Suitcases are inefficient and the best way to carry luggage is on your back. In Nepal, mountain porters use a special basket, hanging from a head strap. Most people, though, need a rucksack with padded shoulder straps and a padded hip belt. With a good rucksack a fit man or woman should be able to carry 20 kilograms with reasonable comfort. For a long trek in the mountains it is sometimes necessary to carry more, maybe as much as 30 kilograms. The rucksack is the mountaineer's home on his back, containing tent, food, stove, sleeping bag, climbing gear and so on, everything he needs to survive in the mountains.

Sleeping bags

After a long day's climb on a cold mountain face, happiness is a warm sleeping bag. The best sleeping bags for mountaineering are made from a thin nylon shell filled with down. Down, the tiniest, softest feathers, is collected from duck or goose nests. No man-made fibre is

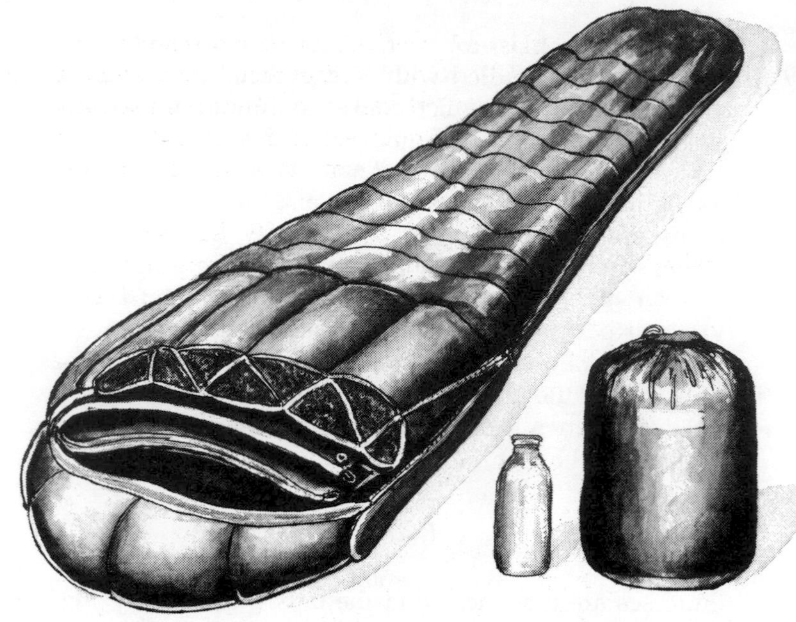

as warm for its weight. The other advantage of down is that it can compress into a tiny space. You can squash a sleeping bag into a small sack during the day but when you pull it out for the night the down compartments fill with air and fluff up into a thick insulating layer.

Stoves

Mountaineers, like sailors and other explorers, need to know how to operate stoves. Many mountain forests have run out of dead wood, and to avoid cutting down live trees expeditions have to carry in fossil fuels, like paraffin and gas. In any case, there is no wood above the treeline.

There are two main types of stove. Pressure stoves burn liquid fuels, like paraffin or petrol. They burn very fast and hot, but the fuel can be awkward, smelly and messy to transport. On difficult bivouacs,* cramped on a ledge or squashed into a tiny tent, mountaineers usually use a lightweight gas stove. The gas, usually a mixture of propane and butane, comes in small pressurized cylinders. One cylinder normally lasts one or two nights' cooking.

Until recently mountaineers usually left the empty cylinders in the mountains but now we carry down the empty cylinders for disposal. The best method is to hammer them flat, burn them to remove all the preserving paint, then bury the flattened metal in the ground to rust away.

Tents

A good mountain tent has to keep out wind, rain and snow; but it also has to allow the moisture produced by people breathing and cooking to escape. The best tents have two layers. The inner layer 'breathes', letting out any vapour. The outer layer – the flysheet – is completely weatherproof, keeping out wind and snow. However, because it is weatherproof it tends to trap moisture inside. When the temperature drops, the moisture freezes, forming a thick layer of frost on the inside of the flysheet. But the occupants stay dry and warm inside the breathable inner tent.

Tents come in all shapes and sizes, but these days the most popular ones for mountains are dome-shaped. Thin metal poles fit into sleeves in the nylon material, stretching it into a firm dome shape. A dome tent for two people usually weighs about 3 kilograms. However, when weight is crucial we sometimes make do with a light single-layer, semi-breathable tent. It is not ideal because the fabric tends to clog up with frost, but it is better than nothing. When Reinhold Messner* soloed Everest* in 1980, his special mini dome tent weighed under two kilograms.

CLOUD PIERCER

Long before white men came to New Zealand, the local Maori people called the highest mountain Aorangi, which means Cloud Piercer. To the Maoris it is still the Cloud Piercer, but its official name is now Mount Cook, after Captain Cook, the great sailor and navigator, who was the first European to see the peak, in 1770. Until recently Mount Cook was 3764 metres high, but in 1991 a gigantic chunk of ice fell from the summit, starting a huge avalanche* and leaving it a few metres lower!

COL

Most people who climb Everest* start the final ascent from the South Col, which is a great dip in the ridge between Everest and the South Peak, Lhotse. On the other side of the mountain there is a similar dip called the North Col, between Everest and the North Peak, Changtse.

Col, like so many mountain terms, is a French word. It means 'neck', but is also used to describe the dip in a ridge, which is

often a narrow passage, like a neck, forming a pass* through the mountains. In the French Alps the famous passes are all called col – Col de Liseran, Col de Lauteret, Col St Bernard and so on.

CONDOR

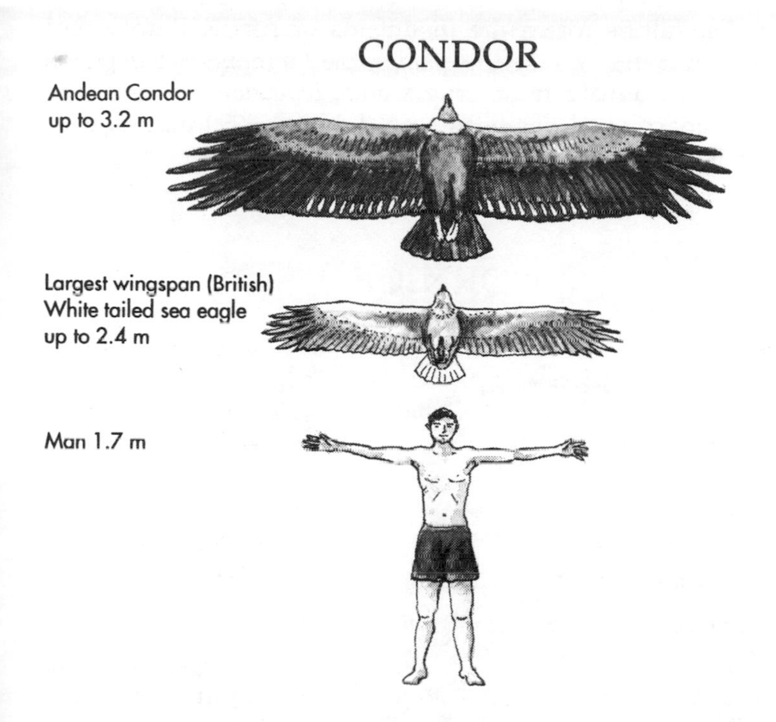

High in the Andes, in South America, lives the world's largest flying bird, the condor. The condor is a species of vulture and it soars high above the mountains, searching for dead animals. Its wingspan – the distance from wingtip to wingtip – is over 3 metres; when it flies overhead it sounds almost like an aeroplane. The air whistles through the spread tips of its immense wings. It is these sensitive wing tips that control the condor's flight, as it glides at speeds of up to 95 kph, travelling huge distances in its search for meat. The wandering albatross has a larger wingspan but is a smaller bird.

In North America there is a slightly smaller condor – the Californian condor – now in danger of extinction: only about thirty birds remain in a forest reserve. It is said that, like the ravens at the Tower of London, on the day the last condor leaves California the country is doomed.

A similar vulture roams the mountains of Africa, Europe and Asia: the Lammergeier. Like the condor, the Lammergeier depends on air currents to make its soaring flights. It has an extraordinary breathing capacity and has been seen flying at 9000 metres, over the summit of Everest.

CORNICE

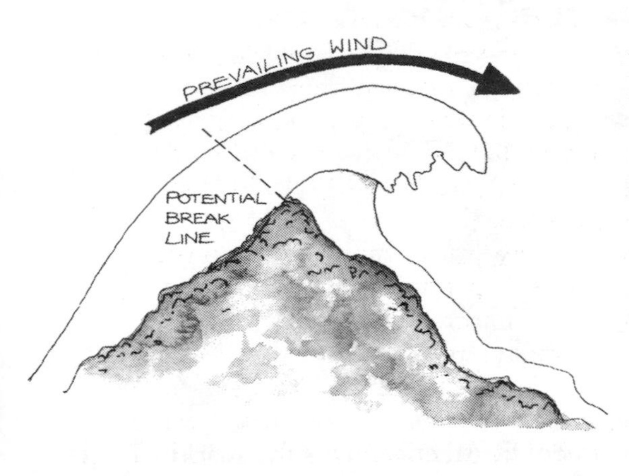

In mountain country the wind usually blows from the same direction. When it hits an exposed ridge it blows the snow off the crest. Gradually, flake by flake, the snow builds up on the far side of the ridge, forming a jutting overhang called a cornice. Cornices sometimes stick out several metres into the air. Often they curl right over like giant creamy meringues. They look magical and beautiful but they are highly dangerous. If you are climbing a corniced ridge, especially in misty weather, you must keep well back from the edge, as the slightest vibration can snap off the fragile overhangs. In hot weather cornices sometimes break off by themselves. When a big one breaks it sounds like a bomb exploding and, as it crashes down the far side of the mountain, may start avalanches.*

CRAMPON see CLIMBING GEAR

CRAWLING TO SAFETY

There have been times when shepherds, hunters or climbers, caught by bad weather in the mountains, have become so weak that they end up crawling on their hands and knees. On other occasions, climbers have just pushed themselves too hard: when Hermann Buhl* reached the summit of Nanga Parbat, the seventh highest mountain in the world, exhaustion forced him to crawl. Others have had to crawl because of accidents. Perhaps the most dramatic mountain crawl of all involved the British mountaineer, Joe Simpson, in 1985. He was in the Andes, in Peru, with his friend Simon Yates. They climbed a difficult new route up a mountain called Siula Grande. On the way down from the summit, Simpson slipped, falling backwards and landing badly on one leg, smashing the knee before the rope stopped him falling any further.

The two mountaineers were alone, high on a remote mountain in Peru. There was no possibility of a rescue and to make matters worse it was starting to snow. Yates could have left his friend to die, but he decided to try to get him down. He lowered Simpson, rope-length by rope-length, down an endless ice slope. For Simpson every little twist and bump was agony. For Yates it was an exhausting struggle, lowering the burden of his helpless friend. Then late that afternoon, disaster struck.

In the swirling snow neither man could see a gigantic overhanging ice cliff below them, and Simpson suddenly shot over the edge and dangled in space. There was no more rope to spare. Fifty metres above, Yates was being slowly pushed off his ledge by the avalanches* of snow. The rope was tugging viciously at his waist. After about an hour he knew that he could not hold on any longer. He

could do nothing to save his friend. There was only one solution. He got out his penknife and cut the rope.

Yates managed to descend alone the next day. On the way down he passed the gigantic ice cliff. Below it there was a huge crevasse.* He could see where his friend had plunged into the depths and shouted down into the icy darkness. There was no reply. Back at base camp he felt depressed, finished, guilty, angry that the crevasse had snatched Simpson after all their efforts to get down safely.

However, unknown to Yates, Simpson was still alive. When the rope was cut, he had fallen like a stone, crashing through a snowbridge* and tumbling down the dark chasm of the crevasse. But further down he landed on another snowbridge, which held his weight. He survived that freezing night on his ledge but in the morning he realized, with despair, that there was no way up. A fit climber might just have climbed the glassy walls, but with a broken leg it was impossible. Instead of escaping upwards he descended, abseiling* down his rope, even deeper into the crevasse. Eventually he reached another ledge, and there, at the far end, was a ramp of snow leading up to a high slit in the ice where sunshine poured through. He could escape from his prison!

That day, and for two more days, Joe Simpson crawled back to life. He crawled out of the crevasse, down the remaining slope of the mountain, then all the way down the long glacier,* dodging more treacherous crevasses, and on down slopes of scree,* where he had to hop, stumbling and tripping all the way. He had no food or water. Every move sent pain shooting through his smashed leg. At times he longed to lie down and give up. But he was determined to survive.

On the third day at base camp, Yates and another friend had packed up to leave. First thing in the morning a shepherd would arrive with his mules to take their baggage down to the nearest road. Nothing would be left at the camp. They would return home to give the awful news to Simpson's parents. In the middle of the night they were

suddenly woken by an extraordinary sound, half wail, half croak, outside their tent. They rushed outside and there, lying on the ground in the darkness, too weak to talk, was Simpson. If he had arrived just a few hours later it would have been too late.

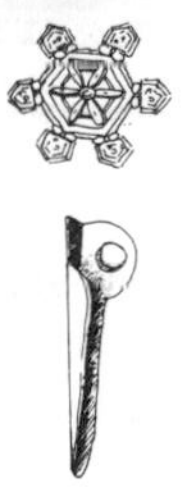

The doctors told Joe Simpson that he could never climb again. But two years later his smashed knee was almost working normally and he was able to start doing some easy climbs. He was also busy writing a book, called *Touching the Void*. When the book was published it was a huge success and was translated into many different languages. It is a gripping account of those desperate days in 1985, when, against all the odds, Joe Simpson crawled back to life.

CREVASSE

It was 1991 and the adventure photographer Leo Dickinson was in his basket at 11,000 metres above sea level, making the first ever balloon flight over Everest* with the Australian pilot Chris Dewhirst. Thousands of metres beneath him a glacier* snaked its way down the mountain, its smooth white surface cut by dark slits, visible even from that altitude. Dickinson was staring through his viewfinder, straight down into the gaping mouths of crevasses.

Those crevasses on Everest are similar to crevasses that split glaciers all around the world. Glaciers are on the move all the time. It may only be a few metres a year, but they are gradually shifting, sliding downhill, round bends and over humps. Sometimes the underneath of the glacier, where the ice slides over rock, moves at a different speed from the surface. All this movement stresses the ice on the surface, cracking it open. The cracks are called crevasses.

A crevasse can be anything from a few centimetres to many metres wide. Usually it is about 40 metres deep, never more than about 100 metres. Below that the weight of ice is so great that it would be impossible to split open.

People have been crossing glaciers for centuries to travel to high mountain passes.* During the last two hundred years mountaineers have crossed glaciers as part of their sport. During these journeys crevasses can be a constant threat. If the ice is bare, they present no danger, because they can be seen clearly and avoided. However, when a glacier is covered by a blanket of snow, the mouths of the crevasses are often smoothed over and hidden. The snowbridge* covering a crevasse may be just half a metre thick, too fragile to support a person's weight.

Mountaineers learn to recognize crevassed areas. Often a slight dip in the snow will give away a crevasse. Nevertheless they are not always obvious and it is easy to make a mistake. Every mountaineer has experienced moments, walking across smooth snow, when his or her foot suddenly shoots down into a concealed hole. A few moments later there is a distant sound like broken glass as pieces of snow and ice tinkle in the darkness far below. Mountaineers are taught always to rope together on snow-covered glaciers, just in case. That way, if people do fall into a crevasse, it is possible to save them from injury or death.

CRYSTALS

Next time it is snowing, catch some snowflakes on a piece of dark cloth. If you look carefully you will see that each flake is actually a star-shaped crystal. Snow crystals change and vary continually and no two crystals are ever identical, but each crystal always forms a hexagon, a six-sided pattern.

The mountains themselves are sometimes like crystals, huge, magical crystals sparkling in the deep blue sky.

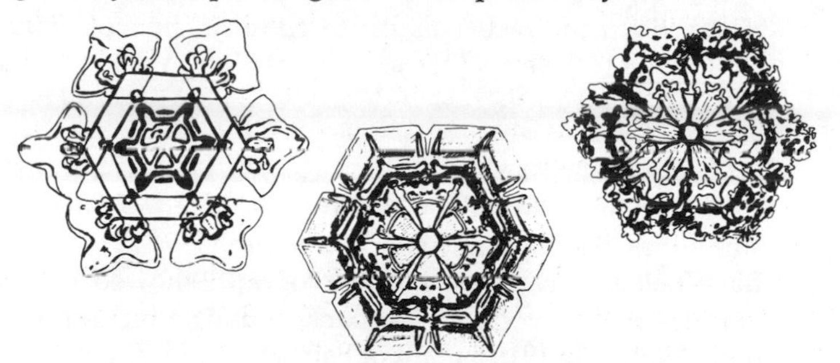

DEATH ZONE

Nothing survives for long in the 'Death Zone' above 8000 metres. There is not enough oxygen in the air to support life. Mountain birds like choughs and ravens sometimes fly up there, but they don't stay for long. The first humans to climb that high were British mountaineers who made the first attempt on Mount Everest* in 1922. They discovered that at such high altitude even the simplest tasks, like turning over in bed, or putting on a boot, require enormous effort. When it comes to moving, you often have to take three or four breaths to every step. (See also THIN AIR.)

DENALI

The highest mountain in North America rises in the far northern state of Alaska. The local American Indians have always called it Denali, which means 'the Great One'. It is a gigantic mountain with two summits. The highest – the south summit – is 6194 metres. Compared to many peaks in the Himalaya*, that is not particularly high, but the base of Denali is almost at sea level. Because it is so far north, near the Arctic, it is probably colder than any Himalayan peak.

In 1897 white Americans renamed Denali Mount McKinley, after the twenty-fourth president of the United States. Soon the race was on to climb it. In those days it could take ten weeks just to reach its foot, walking, skiing and sledging through a wilderness of forests, rivers and glaciers.*

One of the explorers in the race was Frederick Cook. In 1906 he claimed to have reached the top and published his summit photograph in his book, *To the Top of the Continent*. But Cook was careless. His photograph showed the faint impression of a rock in the background, which appeared much higher. In 1910 a team of Fairbanks miners proved that Cook was a hoaxer when they came back with their own photograph of 'Fake Pake', showing it to be nowhere near the summit of Denali. Two years later the Fairbanks team returned to the mountain and claimed the first ascent. However it was only in 1913 that Archdeacon Stuck's team finally reached Denali's highest point. From the south summit they saw the Fairbanks miners' flag on the lower north summit.

Nowadays climbers usually arrive in small aeroplanes, which land with skis on one of the immense glaciers that surround Denali. It is easier to reach the mountain but the climb is never straightforward. Even in summer the temperatures are well below zero and storms are common. Climbers often get frostbite* and many suffer from altitude sickness* when they try to climb too high too fast.

CATHERINE DESTIVELLE

Rock climbing* can make spectacular television viewing. One of the most popular climbing films showed a young Frenchwoman climbing difficult overhanging cliffs, hundreds of metres above the ground, without a rope, relying on the skill in her hands and feet.

Catherine Destivelle was born in Paris in 1960 and from the age of five she climbed on the sandstone rocks at Fontainebleau, just outside Paris. At seventeen she was known as one of the best rock climbers in the world. In recent years she has tackled some of the world's most famous mountains.

The Trango Tower is a great steeple of granite in Pakistan. In 1990 Destivelle climbed one of the most challenging routes up it with the American climber Jeff Lowe. They had to tackle difficult rock climbing at high altitude, where the air contains less oxygen (see THIN AIR). The following year Destivelle achieved what Walter Bonatti* had nearly thirty years earlier: she climbed a difficult new route on the Dru, in the French Alps,* completely alone. She spent nine days alone on the mountain, sleeping on a hanging Portaledge,* which she had to drag up the sheer wall. At one point she fell 10 metres through the air before her ropes held her.

In 1992 Destivelle did her first big winter climb. She chose the famous North Face of the Eiger,* in Switzerland. The first winter ascent had taken six days. Destivelle climbed it alone in just seventeen hours. Although there are many competent female mountaineers, it is still unusual for a woman to attempt such a difficult solo climb. Mountaineering is still dominated by men, but Catherine Destivelle has proved that women can be just as strong.

DEHYDRATION see ALTITUDE SICKNESS

DESERTS

People sometimes imagine that deserts are all flat, monotonous expanses of bare sand, yet many of the world's deserts are mountainous. Perhaps the most famous desert mountain of all is Mount Sinai where, as we are told in the Old Testament of the Bible, Moses received the Ten Commandments during the Flight from Egypt. In Africa, the Tibetis mountains rise from the deserts of Chad. In Chile ancient extinct volcanoes, with snow on their summits, rise from the Atacama desert, one of the driest deserts in the world. In Asia, desert mountains stretch across Iraq, Iran, Afghanistan and Pakistan and north to Kazakhstan, Sinkiang and

Tibet.* In summer these desert mountains are blazing hot, in winter icy cold.

The snow that falls on the mountains brings life to the desert. As it melts it forms rivers which cut deep gorges through the dry land below. In many desert areas, like Hunza in Pakistan, the people divert the water from the gorges, using it to irrigate their fields.

DIAMOND COULOIR

One of the most famous ice climbs in the world is in Africa, right on the Equator. It follows a very steep couloir or gully* of ice, that glints like a diamond. In places the ice is nearly vertical and the couloir was only climbed for the first time in 1973 by the Africans Ranger Thumbe and Phil Snyder. The climb leads to the Gate of the Mists, a gap between the two summits of Mount Kenya. The highest summit (5199 metres) is called Batian and the lower one Nelion. They were named many years ago after famous chiefs of the Kikuyu tribe which lives around Mount Kenya.

DOGS

Dogs have often been put to work in the mountains. In Antarctica the Norwegian explorer Roald Amundsen used huskies to pull his sledges up the Queen Maud mountains on his journey to the South Pole. In the Alps a famous mountain pass* called the St Bernard was once patrolled by huge dogs. The monks at a nearby monastery used to send out the St Bernard dogs to look for travellers who were lost or had collapsed in the snow. Each dog carried on its collar a small barrel of brandy to revive the weak traveller.

St Bernards are huge, powerful animals. However, the Alsatian is usually used nowadays by mountain rescue teams to find people buried in avalanches.*

The most famous mountaineering dog was a mongrel born in the

Swiss Alps in 1865. She looked rather like a dachshund, with a touch of beagle and terrier, and was bought by a local mountain guide, who took her the following year over a high glacier pass called the Tschingel pass. After that first climb she was always known as Tschingel. In 1868 the guide gave her to a well-known English mountaineer, the Reverend W. A. B. Coolidge. During the next ten years she accompanied Coolidge each summer in the Alps, making sixty-six major ascents. In 1869, after climbing Switzerland's highest mountain, Monte Rosa, she was elected an honorary member of the Alpine Club in London.

Tschingel enjoyed climbing as much as her master and when she climbed Mont Blanc* she reached the summit before the rest of the party. Her only real problem was cutting her paws on sharp rocks, and Coolidge tried to persuade her to wear special leather paw pads but she always pulled them off. In the end her own paws became extremely tough. She was particularly good at sensing hidden crevasses,* and she was usually sent out in front on glaciers,* roped by her collar to the rest of the party. Her favourite drinks during climbs were cold tea and red wine.

Tschingel had to give up climbing in old age, when her teeth fell out and she became almost blind. She spent the rest of her life resting peacefully by her master's fireside in England.

DOLOMITES

Dolomite is a type of limestone. In northern Italy a range of mountains is made from this rock. They are called the Dolomites.

The Dolomites are famous for their huge vertical cliffs, many of them over 1000 metres high. Rock climbers* love the thrill of climbing their exposed walls, enjoying the giddy drop into space. Because the rock is limestone, which contains many nutrients and forms countless cracks and hollows, alpine flowers* are often to be found nestling in the cliffs. Between the peaks lie beautiful woods and meadows. In winter, when they are carpeted in snow, these slopes make excellent ski runs. However, there are now so many ski lifts in the Dolomites that people have become depressed by all the pylons and cables littering the countryside and are campaigning to prevent the construction of any more lifts.

DOMES

The best mountains are like beautiful buildings: they are decorated with pillars, buttresses, towers and steeples. Some are like great rounded domes and one of the most dramatic is in the Yosemite National Park, in California. One side of this granite dome

Half Dome in Yosemite National Park, California

is a rounded hump. Every year hundreds of visitors climb up the smooth slope using a fixed cable handrail. However, the other side is very different. Thousands of years ago it was cut away by the giant glacier* that carved out the Yosemite valley, leaving a great vertical precipice 600 metres high. The mountain is naturally called Half Dome.

EDELWEISS

In the highest meadows of Europe and Asia grows a flower like a star, with tiny leaves of soft white felt. The Austrians call it edel-weiss (pronounced aydle-vice) and it means precious-white. The edelweiss is the symbol of the Austrian Alpine Club.

EIGER see OGRES

EIGHT THOUSAND METRES

There are fourteen mountains in the world with summits above 8000 metres. They are all in the Karakoram and Himalayan ranges in Asia. One, Nanga Parbat, lies entirely in Pakistan; five, including K2,* lie on the Pakistan–Sinkiang border; seven, including Everest,* are on the Nepal–Tibet border; Kangchenjunga is on the Nepal–Sikkim border; and Xixabangma lies completely in Tibet. The five highest are Everest (8874 metres), K2 (8612 metres), Kangchenjunga (8595 metres), Lhotse (8501 metres) and Makalu (8470 metres). These five were all climbed in the space of two years between 1953 and 1955.

Only two people have made first ascents of more than one 8000-metre peak. Hermann Buhl* made the first ascent of Nanga Parbat in 1953 and Broad Peak in 1957. His partner on Broad Peak was Kurt Diemberger, who went on to make the first ascent of Dhauligiri in 1960.

The first person to climb all fourteen 8000-metre mountains was the Italian mountaineer, Reinhold Messner,* who devoted many years and numerous attempts to these giant peaks. He started with Nanga Parbat in 1970 and finished with Lhotse, in 1986. A year later the Polish mountaineer Jerzy Kukuczka completed all fourteen peaks.

EL CAPITAN

Hundreds of thousands of years ago immense glaciers* flowed down from the Sierra mountains in California, gouging and carving the granite crust of the earth. The glaciers have long since melted away, but they have left their mark on California, particularly in Yosemite. The Yosemite valley is one of the natural wonders of the world, a great canyon with waterfalls tumbling down the walls on either side. The biggest precipice in the canyon is El Capitan, the Chieftan.

Parachutists have jumped from the top of El Capitan, head first into the valley, a vertical drop of 885 metres. Many parts of the wall are overhanging and from a distance El Capitan looks completely smooth. With a telescope, however, you can just make out ripples, flakes, cracks and chimneys* in the rock. After a while you will probably also notice tiny ant-like figures making their way up these lines in the rock.

The first people ever to climb El Capitan were Warren Harding, Wayne Merry and George Whitmore. They reached the top in 1958, after several attempts, taking a total of forty-seven days spread over seventeen months. Their route, which follows the front edge of El Capitan, is called 'The Nose'.

Since 1958 many other routes have been climbed on El Capitan, all of them with the aid of pitons, bongs and other gadgets hammered into cracks in the rock. Occasionally on blank sections, climbers drilled holes for bolts. Then in 1988, two Americans climbed one route, Salathe Wall, using all these gadgets only for protection, clipping in the ropes to hold them if they fell. But the actual climbing was done completely 'free': they got up those great vertical and overhanging walls using just the skill in their hands and feet.

It took the Americans Paul Piana and Todd Skinner many days to free-climb Salathe Wall. Each night they slept on their hanging Portaledge.* By the end their fingertips were so worn that they had to bind their skin with Superglue. On the last day, finishing up their food, Paul Piana dropped a carrot. Down in the forest a woman was enjoying a peaceful picnic when she suddenly felt a sharp blow on the shoulder. She let out a yell and clutched her bruised shoulder. Turning round, she saw the carrot lying on the ground beside her. It had fallen 900 metres clear through the air.

EQUATOR

A famous explorer called Bill Tilman wrote a book called *Snow on the Equator*. It tells the story of his adventures on the snow mountains of East Africa, in particular Mount Kenya, which sits right on the equator. Although it is very hot at the equator, with no proper winter, snow can still exist if the land rises high enough above sea level. (The temperature drops 1°C for every 300 metres you climb.) The highest mountain in New Guinea, Puncak Jaya,* is very close to the equator but has a glacier* on its summit. In South America the snow-covered summit of Cotopaxi is only 65 kilometres from the equator.

EROSION

Mountains appear massive, solid and unchanging, but they are wearing away all the time. This process is called erosion.

Erosion helped create the mountain shapes that we see today. Glaciers* gouged out the sides of the mountains. Wind,* snow and rain shaped the ridges and gullies.* Ice, expanding inside cracks, continues to split open the rocks. On the famous rock tower of the Dru, in the French Alps, every few years a great slice of granite weighing thousands of tonnes crashes into the valley.

The highest mountains on Earth – the Himalaya* – are also some of the youngest. There you can see erosion working constantly, made worse by people, particularly in the kingdom of Nepal. In the last fifty years the population has doubled and as all those extra people need land to grow food, they cut down trees. But it is the trees that hold the steep hillsides together and once they are gone, the earth is easily washed away by the monsoon rains. When the thin topsoil has gone, the rocks underneath start to slide.

In some of the steep-sided Swiss Alpine valleys, trees are being killed by acid rain, leaving the villages with no protection from landslides and avalanches.

Hill-walkers' boots also cause erosion. In the English Lake District, for example, hill-walking is so popular that in some places visitors are wearing away the hillside, leaving ugly scars. One successful answer to the problem is to build new solid paths with heavy rocks set firmly in the hillside.

Above: Tibetan lady. She is wearing Tibetan turquoise and imported Italian coral. Her amazing skin texture is produced by apricot kernel oils, grown locally and used as a moisturizer.

Above: Terraced fields carved out of the steep mountainside in Nepal. Millet is growing in the tiny strips of fields. Three of the cows are water buffaloes, which produce thick creamy milk.

Above: Sherpa in the Annapurna Himal carrying telegraph poles of, maybe, three times his own weight.

Bottom Left: The famous tea gardens on the hillside at Darjeeling, in north-east India. Fifty km away, the permanent snows of the Himalaya seem to float in the sky.

Bottom Right: Houses in Dzong (Jong), with prayer flags sending prayers to the sky where the gods live. The colours are from rocks. Dzong is only half a mile from the Tibetan border and is the ancient capital of the region.

Above Left: Everest from the North.

Above Right: The famous view of the Matterhorn, seen from the Zermatt valley in Switzerland. Edward Whymper's party made the first ascent of the mountain in 1865, climbing the ridge up the centre. On the right is the shadowy North Face, which was not climbed until 1931, when Franz and Toni Schmid made the first ascent.

Middle: Adam's Peak in Sri Lanka is sacred to Buddhists. Here you can see its shadow stretching away to the lowlands beyond.

Bottom Left: Annapurna in the Nepalese Himalaya.

Bottom Right: Mount Fuji in Japan with Gotemba in the foreground.

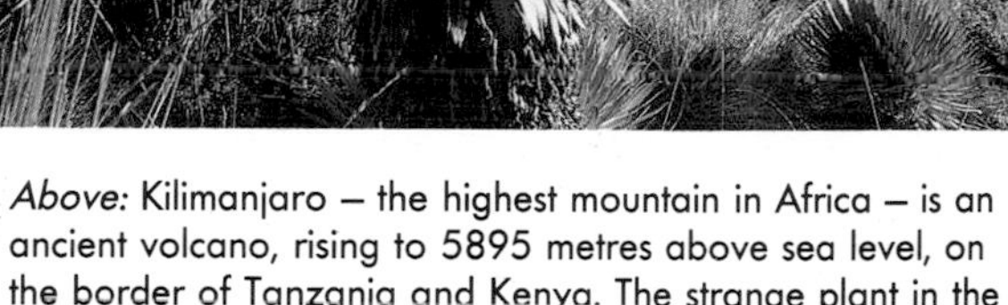

Above: The North Wall of the Eiger soars 1500 metres high, the biggest mountain wall in the Alps.

Above: Kilimanjaro – the highest mountain in Africa – is an ancient volcano, rising to 5895 metres above sea level, on the border of Tanzania and Kenya. The strange plant in the foreground is a giant lobelia, about a metre high.

Middle: Machhapuchhare in Nepal: the sacred 'fishtail' mountain.

Bottom Left: K2, the world's second highest mountain, is much harder to climb than Everest. This is the North Face, seen from Chinese Sinkiang.

Bottom Right: Mont Blanc, the white mountain of Chamonix, is the highest peak in the European Alps.

Above: Avalanche! The author photographed this one from 4 km away, while climbing on Everest.

Left: The Rosenlaui Glacier in the Swiss Alps tumbles from the summit of the Wetterhorn. On the left is the sharp rubble ridge of a lateral moraine. In recent years the glacier ice has receded, leaving bare polished rocks below the tongue.

Above Left: Dick Renshaw climbing a vertical ice cliff in the Himalaya. The cliff is part of a 'hanging glacier', a glacier stuck on the side of a mountain.

Above Right: Dangerous cornices, fragile overhangs of snow formed by the wind, bulging out over the left side of this ridge near the summit of Rajrambha, in the Indian Himalaya.

Below: The Canadian Paul Teare standing behind a glacier table on the Rongbuk Glacier, near the North Face of Everest. The rock, weighing at least a tonne, is balanced on a pillar of ice.

Above: Organizing sixty yak-loads of luggage – supplies and equipment to last three months – for the walk-in to Everest base camp.

Middle: Paul Teare relaxing in his lightweight mountain dome tent, during the walk-in to Everest, while Tibetan porters make do with their traditional heavy tents.

Bottom Left: The author's frostbitten toes, two months after climbing Everest, ready for amputation.

Bottom Right: A luxurious snowcave cut into a huge snowdrift, on the Antarctic island of South Georgia. The author and his team spent a total of twenty-three days living in this cave.

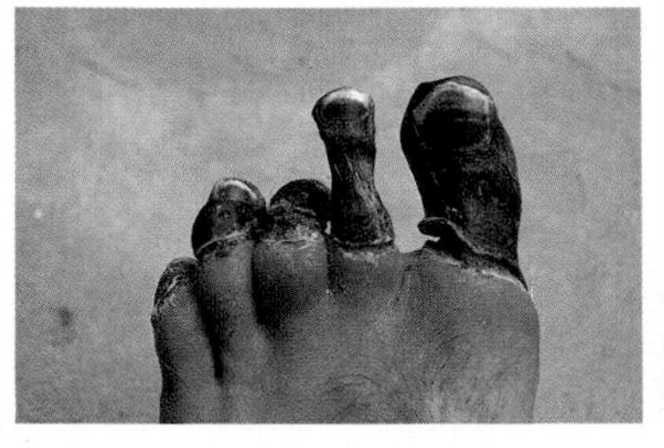

Above Left: Catherine Destivelle, practising big-wall climbing on Moses Tower, in Utah, North America. She is relaxing on a Portaledge, a collapsible platform which can be hauled up a wall to provide an instant ledge for the night.

Above Right: Inside a crevasse on Everest.

Right: Walking up the gritty ice surface of a glacier in South Georgia, skirting round the great chasm of a crevasse.

Bottom: Crossing a reliable snowbridge over a crevasse in the Peruvian Andes.

Above Left: The author climbing on the sandstone cliffs of Table Mountain, above Cape Town, at the tip of South Africa.

Above Right: Ayers Rock in Australia. The biggest single monolith in the world.

Below: The Chamonix Aiguilles in the glow of the setting sun. Left to right: L'Aiguille de Blaitière, L'Aiguille des Ciseaux, L'Aiguille du Fou, Le Dent du Caiman, Le Dent du Crocodile.

EUROPEANS

The sport of mountaineering started in Europe. It was only during this century that people from other continents began to climb mountains for fun. Even today most mountaineers come from a handful of richer countries, where people have time and money for leisure and holidays.

EVEREST

Far from any city, hidden among a maze of peaks and glaciers* on the Nepal–Tibet frontier, stands a great mountain. For centuries the local people called it Chomolungma or Sagamartha, which mean Mother Goddess of the Earth. Then in the nineteenth century British surveyors started to map and measure the Himalayan* peaks from their viewpoints in India. They gave the important peaks numbers and as they did not know that Chomolungma had a name they called it 'Peak XV'.

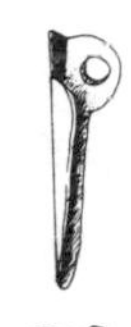

In 1852 the surveyors discovered from their calculations that Peak XV was 29,029 feet (8848 metres) high, higher than any other mountain in the world. (Modern satellite measurements put it at 8874 metres.) They decided to name it after a famous retired director of the Survey of India, Sir George Everest.

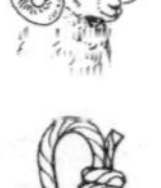

It was only much later, in 1921, when a British expedition arrived to try to find a route to the summit, that they discovered its real name, Chomolungma. The British explorers had to walk from India, up through Sikkim to Tibet,* on the north side of the mountain. In those days no foreigners were allowed into Nepal, on the south side, and even getting into Tibet required years of negotiation with the Tibetan government. That first expedition in 1921 discovered a possible route up the north side of Everest. However, between 1922 and 1938 seven attempts were made without anyone reaching the summit. At least we

think that no one reached the summit. But it is just possible that in 1924 George Mallory* and Andrew Irvine did.

In 1924 Colonel Norton reached 8600 metres above sea level in the death zone.* (See also THIN AIR.) Compared to a modern climber he had poor equipment and he was not using bottled oxygen. Norton turned round because he knew that if he carried on he would not get back to his top camp before dark. His high point remained a record for climbing without oxygen for fifty-four years.

During the Second World War no one attempted Everest, and soon after it ended the Chinese invaded Tibet, closing the frontier to all foreigners. However, at about the same time the King of Nepal decided to allow foreigners to explore the south side of Everest, which is how a British expedition came to find the route up the hidden valley called the Western Cwm in 1951. The following year a Swiss team climbed further up this route to the South Col and almost to the summit. The French had permission to try in 1954, but the British were allowed one more attempt in 1953.

The British expedition of 1953 was led by Colonel John Hunt. Like all the previous expedition leaders he planned a series of camps up the mountain and employed local Sherpa* porters to help carry the loads, which included heavy cylinders of oxygen* and breathing masks to be used high on the mountain. He was also helped enormously by the experience of the Swiss the previous year. This year, on 26 May, two British climbers, Evans and Bourdillon, reached the south summit of Everest, only 80 metres below the top; but their oxygen was running out and they had to make the agonizing decision to descend. Three days later it was the New Zealander, Edmund Hillary,* and the Nepalese Sherpa, Tenzing Norgay,* who had the honour of climbing the last difficult ridge. To this day, the final cliff below the summit is known as the Hillary Step.

In 1953 two mountaineers finally stood on top of the world. By 1992 over 400 people had reached it. There are now many different routes up the mountain. A British

expedition led by Chris Bonington was first up the South-West Face in 1975. A Slovenian expedition climbed the West Ridge in 1979. The old pre-war route from the north was finally climbed by the Chinese, and the gigantic East Face by an American team in 1983.

One of the most exciting events was in 1978 when Reinhold Messner* and Peter Habeler beat Colonel Norton's record and became the first to reach the summit without using bottled oxygen. Between 1978 and 1993 about another fifty people reached the summit without using oxygen; but it is a risky business and the majority of climbers carry up the heavy cylinders.

The first female to climb Everest was Japanese, Junko Tabei, in 1975; the first woman to reach the top without oxygen was the New Zealander Lydia Bradey in 1988. The person who has been up most often is the local Sherpa climber, Ang Rita; by 1992 he had been to the summit seven times, always without oxygen.

One final record. Most routes on Everest start from a base camp at about 5000 metres. In 1991 the Australian climber Tim Macartney-Snape climbed all 8874 metres of Everest, starting at sea level and walking all the way from the Indian ocean 700 kilometres away.

EVEREST WITHOUT OXYGEN

Imagine walking up a long, continuous staircase. For each step you take you must draw in three huge breaths. At first you manage to do twenty steps before stopping to rest. After a while you find you have to stop and rest every ten steps. Then your legs feel so weak that you can only manage two or three steps at a time, before collapsing to rest, panting furiously. That is how it feels to climb Everest without oxygen.*

Most mountaineers on Everest still use oxygen equipment to compensate for the lack of oxygen in the air. (See

also ALTITUDE SICKNESS and THIN AIR.) It makes the climb easier and a lot safer. Nevertheless some people prefer to attempt the mountain without this artificial aid. In 1988 I had a chance to try a new route up the East Face of Everest with three American climbers. With no support team, it was impossible for the four of us to carry up heavy oxygen equipment as well as all our tents, food, stoves and so on. In any case we wanted to see if we could manage without. Our new route finished on the South Col at 8000 metres, but from there we still had another 874 metres to climb up the normal route to the summit. Paul Teare felt ill and was worried about altitude sickness,* so he made the wise decision to turn back. That left three of us still hoping to reach the summit.

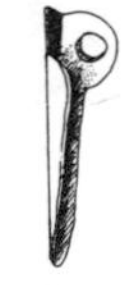

On the final day we discovered just how hard it is to do anything above 8000 metres without oxygen equipment. It took three hours just to put on our clothes, boots and crampons. On the final climb our average height gain was only 50 metres an hour. Sometimes we were having to stop and rest after every single step, gasping and desperate to get more oxygen into our lungs, so that the blood could transport it to our feeble muscles.

Oxygen starvation affects the brain as well as muscles. At about 8700 metres Ed Webster hallucinated, seeing imaginary Tibetan monks, in orange and purple robes, walking around the summit of Everest. I did not *see* anything but when I was completely alone, ahead of the others, I had a strong feeling that some unknown person was with me. By that stage Webster and Robert Anderson had turned back, only 80 metres from the summit, when clouds began to swirl around the summit ridge. Because I had been slightly faster, I had been able to continue with my imaginary companion to the summit, but by the time I started down it was cloudy and the light was fading fast. I was unable to get back to our tents before dark so I had to stop and bivouac* in the open, without a sleeping bag, at 8500 metres.

All through the long shivery night imaginary people joined me on my ledge in the snow, but eventually they disappeared and the long-awaited dawn arrived. I rejoined Ed and Robert that morning, but it took us another three days to descend to base camp. By the time we got down all of us had frostbitten toes and Ed also had frostbite* on his fingers. We were so weak that for two days we lay in our tents, unable to get up and walk.

Other people have managed better without oxygen: a Frenchman called Marc Batard raced to the summit in just 22½ hours from base camp. He was extraordinarily fit and he climbed the easiest route up the mountain, helped by other people's tracks. We were less fit and climbed a difficult new route, which took much longer – five days up and four days down. It was too long to spend at altitude, which is why we became desperately weak. Nevertheless it was a fantastic adventure!

EXPEDITION

An expedition is a journey with a special purpose. A mountaineering expedition may set out to attempt an unclimbed summit, or to try a new route or, perhaps, to explore unknown glaciers.* Usually one person acts as leader and organizer. When he or she chooses a team, it is important to consider how the members will get on with each other after several weeks' stuck together in tents, far from civilization. There are always some squabbles on expeditions, but it is best to keep them to a minimum.

One of the biggest expeditions was Chris Bonington's* to the South-West Face of Everest in 1975. There were ten lead climbers, eight support climbers, two doctors, a television team, cooks, messengers and 60 high-altitude porters to help move supplies up the mountain. The expedition was a great success because everyone worked well together and every tiny detail of this complicated operation was carefully organized.

However, mountaineers usually prefer to work in teams of two or four people. A small expedition is easier to arrange and each person gets a bigger share of the excitement of leading. Small expeditions need fewer supplies and fewer porters to carry them, so they probably have less effect on the fragile mountain environment.

A typical large expedition might employ 300 porters. If they do not carry paraffin, all those porters have to burn wood for their cooking and buy food from local people who may not have much to spare. The climbing team might have as many as twenty foreigners living for weeks in one small area of the mountains. With that number of people it is hard to control pollution and to dispose of all special gear like food packaging, spent batteries and gas cylinders.

EXTREME SKIING

Skiers love the thrill of speeding down steep slopes. Some ski runs feel vertical, but the average angle may be only about 15 degrees; even the hardest runs – black runs – are rarely steeper than 30 degrees.

Extreme skiers are experts who descend much steeper slopes. They ski down the sort of mountain faces that mountaineers normally climb *up*, using ice axes and crampons, slopes where if you

Extreme skiing – slopes up to 70°

Black run – up to 30°

stand upright you can easily touch the slope with your hand. These extreme ski descents are only possible at certain times of the year when a thin layer of snow covers the hard ice. The skier has to come down in a series of very sharp zig-zags, turning all the time, cutting into the surface with the razor-sharp metal edges of his or her skis. A single mistake – and he or she will almost certainly fall to their death.

Many of the top extreme skiers are French, and one of the best-known is Pierre Tardivel. In the French Alps* he skied down the North Face of the Courtes: it is 800 metres high and sections of the face are nearly 70 degrees steep. In 1992 Tardivel joined an expedition to Everest.* With the help of oxygen, he carried his skis to the South Summit, just 80 metres below the main summit. From there he skied down the mountain – the first ski descent of Everest.

FLAMMES DE PIERRE

All over the world people love to give names to their mountains. Near Chamonix, in France, there are some jagged spikes of red granite, called Flammes de Pierre, which means Flames of Stone. In the evening, particularly, they seem to flicker in the sky. It was from the Flames of Stone that Walter Bonatti* started the approach to his great climb on the Dru in 1955.

FRENCH

Many of the words in this book are French: mountain terms like arête, couloir, avalanche, crevasse, crampon, névé and so on. This is probably because the language of mountains was developed in the Alps. Although many parts of the Alps are German- and Italian-speaking, the French region of Mont Blanc has always been popular with mountaineers. The town at the foot of

Mont Blanc, Chamonix, is known as *la capitale mondiale de l'alpinisme*, the world capital of alpinism (or mountaineering).

FRIEND see CLIMBING GEAR

FROSTBITE

If you have ever been really cold, you will probably have experienced numb fingers and toes, which can usually be brought back to life quite quickly by warming them up. You may feel a few moments of burning pain, but then they return to normal.

Fingers and toes become numb because they are furthest from the heart; they are the body's 'extremities'. When the body is threatened by cold it tries to keep the warm blood near its centre to protect the 'core' of vital organs. In extreme conditions the blood is cut off completely from the outside parts, so that they start to die: they become frostbitten.

When a finger is first frostbitten it looks white and waxy. After a day or two it turns purple and large blisters appear. Eventually it turns hard shiny black, like polished ebony, completely without feeling. If the frostbite is not too deep, the finger will recover and after a few weeks the hard black shell will fall off, revealing new flesh and skin underneath. However, in serious cases the whole affected area dies. Eventually it either falls off or has to be amputated.

Mountaineers sometimes get frostbitten, particularly at very high altitudes. Apart from the cold there is an extra problem at altitude: the blood becomes thicker, so its circulation is less effective and the extremities are even more likely to go numb. High-altitude mountaineers try hard to avoid frostbite but occasionally things go wrong. When Maurice Herzog climbed Annapurna in 1950 he lost his gloves near the summit. His hands turned to blocks of wood. The frostbite was so bad that afterwards all his fingers had to be amputated.

In 1988 I was frostbitten when I climbed Everest without oxygen.* I was delayed at the summit and had to bivouac* in the open at 8600 metres, lying on my ledge in the snow, with no sleeping bag. I managed to keep my hands alive by sticking them deep inside my down jacket, but I could not take off my boots to warm up my toes, so they froze. My left foot was lying underneath the right, and it was on the left that the frostbite was worst. Now only the little toe and half of the fourth toe remain on that foot.

FUJI

Mount Fuji is one of the world's most famous volcanoes, a beautiful white-topped cone towering above the plain outside Tokyo. For centuries the Fuji-ko religious sect has worshipped the mountain, which is a symbol of perfection. Each summer, long before people thought of mountaineering, hundreds of pilgrims climbed to the summit, chanting as they ascended in special white robes.

GLACIERS

A hundred thousand years ago much of the Earth was covered by ice. After the last Ice Age, most of this ice sheet melted away. However, parts of the Earth are still covered by ice, in particular the polar regions where the air temperature is usually below freezing, even at sea level. Outside these areas you have to climb high in the mountains to find permanent ice. The ice usually flows down mountain valleys, like huge frozen rivers. These rivers of ice are called glaciers.

There are glaciers in Norway and in the European Alps. In Canada glaciers are to be found in the Rocky mountains, while further north, in the Yukon, the glaciers are immense. Australia has no mountains high enough to support permanent ice, but there are many glaciers in the Southern Alps of New Zealand.

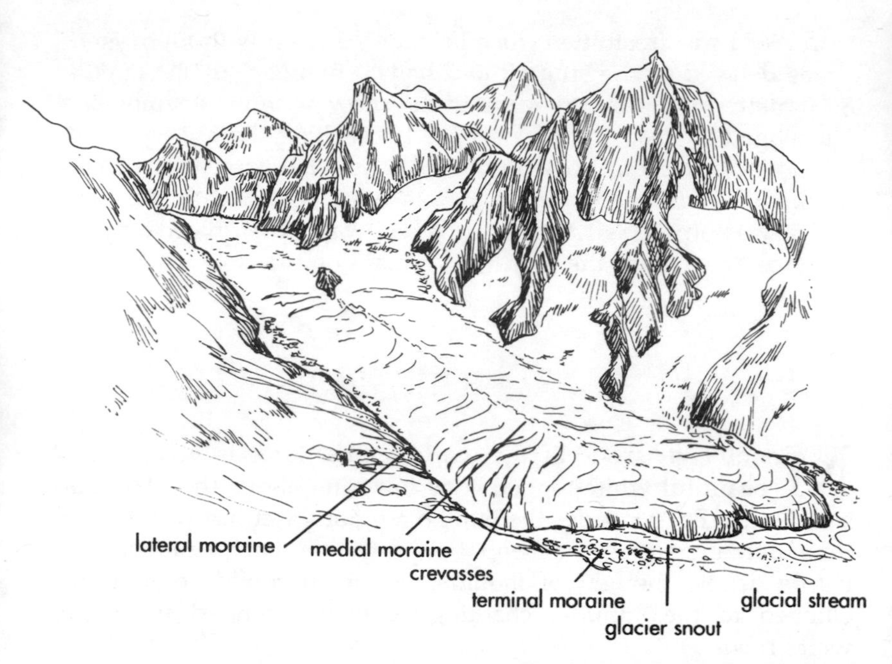

Some glaciers are tiny, just a few hundred metres long. Others run for many kilometres; the longest in the world is probably the Lambert glacier in Antarctica, which flows 400 kilometres through the mountains to an ice shelf floating on the sea.

In the summer glaciers usually melt a little. The upper part may be covered by snow, but lower down bare ice is exposed to the sun. As the ice melts it forms streams and rivers, rushing across the ice surface, sometimes disappearing down vertical tunnels. All the water eventually comes out at the bottom: the 'snout' or 'tongue' of the glacier.

'If they melt every summer,' you may ask, 'why don't glaciers disappear completely?' The answer is that, in many areas, glaciers *are* slowly disappearing, getting smaller each year. However, as they flow down the mountains they are also being fed from above. All the snow that falls on the glaciers is gradually compressed into ice and this new ice keeps the glaciers alive. Many glaciers are in danger of disappearing, as a result of global warming. However, some are so huge that they must remain for many thousands of years. Just to give one example, the Biafo glacier, in Pakistan, is 50 kilometres long. Near the top the ice is over a kilometre thick.

Glaciers are beautiful and magical. They make the mountains special. They form huge snowfields, as smooth as velvet. When they flow over steep ground, they break up into great glittering crystal towers. Their surface cracks up into deep green crevasses.* Like rivers, they form waves and ripples. They are constantly changing, day by day, year by year.

GLACIER TABLE

A photograph in the centre section of this book shows a glacier table, a huge sheet of rock balanced on a column of ice. How did it happen? The rock was one of many littering the surface of the glacier. During the summer tiny rocks and pebbles were heated by the sun so that they melted the ice and sank out of sight. But larger rocks like this one could never heat right through. During the summer the surrounding ice melted down nearly two metres, but the ice beneath the centre of the rock was sheltered from the sun's rays and could not melt so remained as a pillar with the rock balanced on top.

GODS AND GODDESSES

Mountains reach up into the heavens, their summits often lost in swirling clouds. They give out an aura of power and mystery and many people around the world regard mountains as holy places, the home of the gods.

Hundreds of years ago, in the Chilean Andes, high above the Atacama desert, the Incas made sacrifices on some of the highest summits. In Australia the Aborigines worshipped Ayers Rock*. In the Sinai desert, Christian monks still live at the monastery of Santa Katerina, below Mount Sinai, associated with Moses and Jesus. In ancient Greece, Mount Olympus was the throne from which Zeus and his twelve other gods looked down on the world of mortals. Many of the people in the Himalaya are Hindus or Buddhists and for them the most holy mountain of all is Mount Kailas in Tibet.* There are numerous holy mountains, like the highest mountain in India, the 7817-metre Nanda Devi,* the Mother Goddess, whose melting snows and glaciers* feed the waters of the holy river Ganges. In the Buddhist kingdom of Bhutan most of the peaks have never been attempted by foreign climbers because the local people do not want the gods to be disturbed. The people of Tibet have the same feeling for their mountains: whenever you cross a high pass* in Tibet you find prayer flags fluttering in the breeze. Mountains, forests, rocks and lakes . . . the whole country is holy. Like the Indians of North America, the Tibetans have a deep respect for the land, in which lies a lesson for all of us.

GRANITE

Climbers love granite. It is a solid, reliable rock. It forms beautiful slabs, spires and chimneys,* which are a joy to climb.

Granite is an igneous rock, which means that it was formed by intense heat and pressure when the Earth's crust was still melting, and is a mixture of quartz, mica and feldspar crystals. If you crack open a piece of granite it looks mottled, and you can see the different coloured crystals.

From a distance granite usually appears one colour: El Capitan* is grey; Changabang, in India, is a silvery white; Trango Tower, in Pakistan, is golden red, like the granite cliffs at Land's End on the western tip of England.

GULLY

Gullies are giant drains. They are the grooves and channels down which snow and water pour off mountains. For climbers they are often the best way *up* mountains, but only when they are frozen solid. In warm conditions gullies become dangerous because they are the natural drainage channels for falling rocks or snow avalanches.*

Another good word for gully is 'gulch'. Mountaineers also use the French word 'couloir'.

Gully lying between two peaks

HALLUCINATIONS see EVEREST WITHOUT OXYGEN

HEADLAMP see CLIMBING GEAR

HELICOPTER

Fifty years ago when people were injured in the mountains the only way to get them down was to lower them on ropes or carry them on stretchers, which might take several days, or even weeks, and was often painful for the injured person. In some parts of the world it could be a journey of several hundred kilometres to the nearest road.

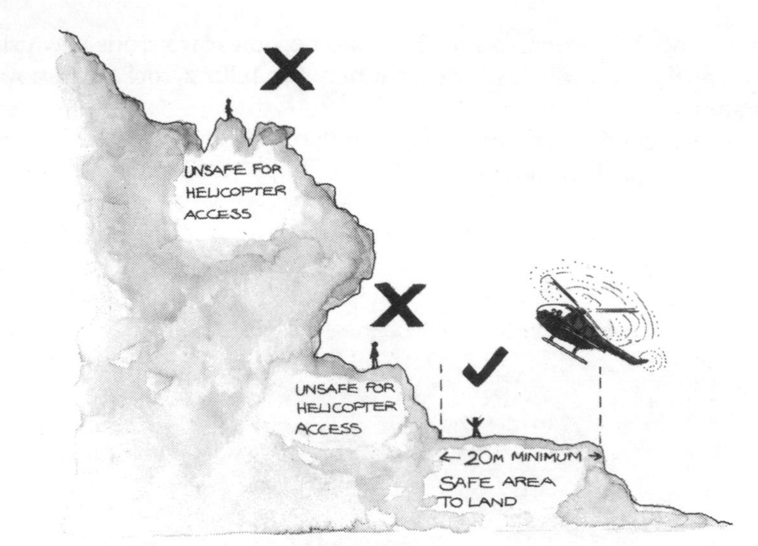

Nowadays helicopters can reach the most extraordinary places: they are equipped to land on tiny spaces; if necessary they can hover, while a wire is lowered to winch up the injured person. Climbers have been rescued like this from huge precipices such as the North Wall of the Eiger.* Sometimes the rotor blades are whizzing round only a metre of so from the mountain – one tiny mistake and the helicopter crashes, killing everyone. It requires the most skilful flying by highly experienced pilots, who must also be keenly aware of the strange air currents that circulate in mountain areas.

Helicopters are not only used for rescue. They carry building materials to remote mountain farms or food supplies to a mountain hut. If you have enough money, you can hire a helicopter to take you to a distant snowy summit and leave you there for a wonderful ski descent. Photographers hire helicopters for making mountain films.

Because mountain flying is so dangerous the pilot has to be able to see where he is going and cannot fly in thick cloud. There is also an altitude limit: even the lightest helicopters cannot operate much above 6000 metres, where the air becomes too thin* to support them.

In 1992, when I broke both my legs on a Himalayan peak, the Indian Air Force sent a helicopter to pick me up from an isolated glacier* at 5600 metres. If we had been much higher, there would have been no chance of a helicopter rescue and the only hope would have been a long, difficult descent with ropes and stretchers. As it was, the helicopter was operating at the limit of its capability. It was too small to carry a winch, so it had to land on the snow to pick me up. The only flat spot was the ledge we had cut into the slope for our tent and the pilot had to land the helicopter with just one skid resting on the ledge, the rotor blade slicing the air just half a metre from the slope. At sea level, that kind of landing requires enormous skill; at 5600 metres it is an amazing feat. Had the pilot made a single mistake we would all have been killed, but he kept calm and held the helicopter steady while I hauled myself aboard, broken legs flapping behind me. Ten minutes later I was safely down in the valley, thanking the pilot and co-pilot, and thinking what a miraculous machine the helicopter is.

EDMUND HILLARY

At eleven thirty on the morning of 29 May 1953, Edmund Hillary took a photograph that would soon be seen all over the world. It shows Sherpa Tenzing Norgay* dressed in bulky padded down clothing, standing on a mound of snow against a deep blue sky. One arm is raised, holding up an ice axe, tied to which are the flags of India, Nepal and Great Britain. Tenzing and Hillary had just become the first people known to stand on the summit of Everest.*

Edmund Hillary was born in New Zealand, where he learned to climb in the rugged Southern Alps. In 1951 for him a dream came true: he had the chance to visit India, to climb in the Himalaya.* Later that summer he and his New Zealand friends joined British explorer Eric Shipton in Nepal, where they discovered the route up the Khumbu icefall to the Western Cwm of Everest. Two years later Hillary was chosen to join the British attempt to reach the mountain's summit.

Hillary was one of the fittest, strongest and most experienced climbers in the 1953 team and was an obvious choice

Hillary and Tenzing at 27,000 feet on Everest

for the summit. On the day before the attempt, he carried a 29-kilogram rucksack to make the top camp – hard work at sea level, unbelievable at 8500 metres. With the help of oxygen (see THIN AIR) he and Tenzing slept that night in their tiny tent, perched on a snow ledge, higher than anyone had ever slept before. In the morning they left at six thirty. Just below the summit they had to climb a difficult cliff, now called the Hillary Step. An hour later they were on top of the world.

The news of the successful climb reached Britain three days later, just in time for the coronation of Queen Elizabeth II. Later that year Hillary was knighted by the Queen to become Sir Edmund Hillary, but in Nepal, the Sherpa* people who live near Everest call him Bara Sahib, which means the top man or boss man. The Sherpas respect him because he climbed Everest with Tenzing; but what they admire most is all the work he has done since 1953, helping to build schools and hospitals, and planting new forests for the Sherpa people.

HIMALAYA

'In a hundred ages of the gods I could not speak of all the glories of the Himalaya,' wrote one of the old Hindu prophets about the mountains of Himalaya. It is indeed a wonderful natural treasure house, towering above the plains of India. Himalaya comes from two words, *hima* which means snow, and *alaya* which means abode: Abode of Snow.

The Himalaya are fold mountains: they were created by a folding up of the earth's crust. According to scientists, the Earth's crust is made up of shifting 'tectonic plates'. About 100 million years ago a part of the original southern continent, Gondwana, broke away and drifted north at a rate of about 20 centimetres a year. The land that is now India sat on this plate. About 50 million years ago the Indian landmass collided with Tibet, part of the Eurasian plate. It was a gigantic collision and as India ploughed under Tibet, the Himalayan mountain chain was pushed up along the collision line. That is a very simple explanation of how the world's greatest mountain range was created. The Himalaya are some of the youngest mountains in the world: many of the cliffs in Australia were formed 3500 million years ago.

The Himalaya stretch in a great arc for about 2500 kilometres. At its eastern end, the range peters out in the great forests and jungles of Eastern Tibet, Assam and Burma. Its western extremity is marked by the giant bulk of Nanga Parbat, which towers above the Indus river. (In just 20 kilometres Nanga Parbat rises from the Indus at 1000 metres to a summit over 8000 metres above sea level.) North and west of the Indus the mountains march on into the Karakoram and Hindu Kush ranges. North of them lie the great ranges of Central Asia: the Pamirs, Tien Shan, Kun Lun and Altai.

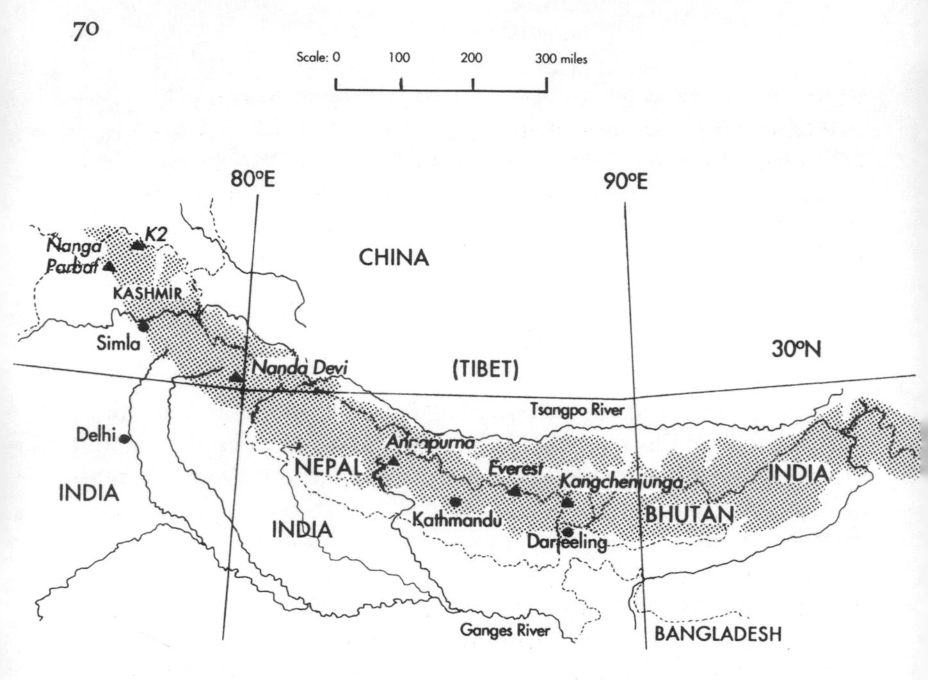

THE HIMALAYAN MOUNTAIN RANGE

The Himalaya are drained by four main rivers: the Indus, Sutlej, Ganges and Brahmaputra. Although they follow different paths through the mountains, diverging for thousands of kilometres, they all start within a few kilometres of the holy Mount Kailas, in Tibet.

HUNZA

Sometimes in whole-food shops you can find packets of dried Hunza apricots. They come from the mountain province of Hunza, in north Pakistan. Until the recent building of the Karakoram Highway,* Hunza was an independent principality, ruled by the Mir of Hunza. For centuries the people lived in isolation, deep among the Karakoram mountains.

Hunza is a huge oasis. Specially built irrigation channels carry the water from glacier* torrents to terraced fields, bringing life to the dry land. Many of these channels are cut out of the rock, hundreds of metres up sheer cliff faces. In the fields below, the people of Hunza grow barley and vegetables. All around the fields there are orchards of fruit and nut trees. In August, every flat rooftop in the villages is carpeted bright orange with thousands of apricots drying in the sun.

HUTS

Shepherds and hunters have always built stone huts high in the mountains, in the summer pastures. For centuries these were the only huts, but now in some places there are also special huts for mountaineers.

The most famous mountain huts are in the European Alps.* They are usually perched on rocky bumps beside glaciers,* safe from avalanches* and shifting ice. Some are so big that they are almost hotels. Mountaineers pay for a meal and hot water and a mattress space in one of the dormitories. Usually a guardian looks after the hut during the spring skiing season and the summer climbing season.

Some of the huts are just tiny emergency shelters, little cabins held to the rock by cables. One of the best known is the Solvay Hut, half-way up the Matterhorn. Perhaps the most unusual mountain hut in the world is in Africa: on Mount Kenya there is a tiny cabin right on top of one of its twin summits.

IBEX

You need very sharp eyes to see them: they keep their distance and their brown-grey fur camouflages them against the rocks. They run and leap along cliffs, long before humans can catch up with them. But sometimes, if you are lucky, you can get close to an ibex.

The ibex is a goat, which lives in the high mountains of Europe and Asia, nibbling alpine plants, grass and lichen. It is a large, heavy animal, with huge beautiful horns, sometimes over a metre long, that sweep back in a great curve. Its hoofs are hard as steel, with soft, hollowed heel pads that cling to rocks like suction pads, enabling the ibex to leap and run over the most terrifying precipices.

Ibex live in herds. When they see danger, they warn each other with a whistling noise. The other common sound they make is the banging and rattling of horns during the mating season when the males fight for mates.

ICE AXE see **CLIMBING GEAR**

ICE HAMMER see **CLIMBING GEAR**

ICEFALL

Imagine a river, flowing in a broad gentle valley. Suddenly the valley narrows. The water is squeezed through the gap and over a great cliff. The result is a waterfall or rapids.

Glaciers* behave in a similar way. When a glacier flows over steep rock, the ice cracks and shatters. Because glaciers flow much more slowly than rivers, the ice only breaks gradually. Sometimes icefalls seem completely still, but often you hear creaking, grinding, gnashing noises. Once in a while a tower of ice collapses with a great crash.

Mount Everest is guarded by an icefall. Those who attempt the mountain from the south must first climb the famous Khumbu icefall. Each year mountaineers fix ropes, marker flags and even ladders up 1000 metres of ice chaos. Each year the route is different. Sometimes it changes from day to day. The Khumbu icefall is a dangerous, frightening place and many climbers have died there, swallowed by the shifting ice.

INCA

For centuries it lay forgotten, overgrown by trees and ferns. Then in 1911 the American archaeologist, Hiram Bingham, rediscovered Machu Picchu, a city built on terraces cut into the side of a mountain, deep in the forests of Vilcabamba, in Peru. Machu Picchu was built by the Incas, who worshipped the sun and built great temples where humans were sacrificed to the sun god. The Inca emperor was able to control a huge area of mountainous land because he had good communications; stone-built paths ran through the most jagged mountain country. Because the Incas did not know about the wheel, messages were carried by runners. Baggage was carried by slower llama* caravans.

Horses were unknown in South America until Spanish soldiers arrived from Europe in the sixteenth century. The Inca people were terrified of these strange creatures and of the *conquistadores* who rode them through their country, searching for gold and silver. In their greed for treasure, the *conquistadores* robbed and destroyed the Inca empire.

Nowadays it is tourists who visit Peru. Many of them come to walk and climb in the Andes mountains, and one of the most popular journeys is the trek to Machu Picchu, the lost city of the Incas.

INDUS

The land to the south of the Himalaya* has always been known as India. The name comes from the river Indus, one of the great rivers of the world, which flows from one of the great mountain ranges, the Karakoram.

Since 1947 most of the Indus has flowed within the new state of Pakistan but the river rises far to the north, in Tibet,* near Mount Kailas. Its waters are the lifeblood of Pakistan.

From its source the Indus flows west through India, then into Pakistan, where it cuts right through the giant mountain chain of the Karakoram. All the melting snow and ice finds its way into the Indus. Earth and rock, scraped and ground up by the glaciers,* also flows into the river. The water is thick and brown with rock dust and in summer it carries 5 million tonnes of sediment a day. This sediment, of rock ground up into a fine powder of different minerals, forms the soil of the rich farmlands in the Punjab.

JET-STREAM WINDS see WINDS

K2

All mountaineers know that K2 is much more difficult to climb than Everest.* Just getting there is hard. From the north it is a long journey through the deserts of Sinkiang. From Pakistan, in the south, it takes ten days to walk from the village of Askole. K2 lies in a savage wilderness of snow, ice and rock, right at the heart of the Karakoram range, far from any road or village.

In the nineteenth century, British surveyors began to measure and map the Karakoram mountains, labelling them 'K' for Karakoram – K1, K2, K3 and so on. Most now have local names: K1, for instance, is called Masherbrum. However, because K2 is so remote and local people never talked about it much – until foreign explorers and mountaineers arrived on the scene – it has no established local name and is still called K2.

By chance, K2 turned out to be the second highest mountain in the world, 8612 metres above sea level. It is a magnificent mountain, a huge pyramid towering far above all the neighbouring peaks. It is everything that mountaineers dream about. But those dreams can be dangerous, because the pyramid is often blasted by powerful winds and storms. It is steep all the way and there is no easy way down during a storm.

In 1939 a German-American climber, Fritz Wiessner, almost reached the summit of K2, but had to turn back just 200 metres from the top. It was getting dark and his Sherpa* companion, Pasang Dawa Lama, refused to go on, terrified of the mountain spirits that might attack them in the dark.

It was an Italian expedition that made the first successful ascent of K2 in 1954. After weeks of hard work Lino Lacedelli and Achille Compagnoni reached the summit at dusk on 31 August. They used oxygen* bottles on their climb, but nowadays most expeditions to K2 do not, because it is too expensive to have them carried such a long way from the road.

The second ascent of K2 was in 1977. Since then many new routes have been climbed up the mountain – but there have been disasters. During the summer of 1986, thirteen people died on K2. Two were killed by an avalanche,* one fell in a crevasse,* one was hit by a rock, others slipped and fell down the mountain, exhausted by the shortage of oxygen at the summit.

During the final tragedy seven people were trapped in a storm on their way down from the summit. Day after day

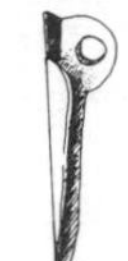

the snow piled up around their tiny tents. Julie Tullis and Alan Rouse, the first two Britons to reach the summit of K2, died in their tents. After six days, when the storm finally ended, the others started down. Two Austrians, Immitzer and Wieser, collapsed after a few metres. They had no strength left and lay helpless in the snow. The other two Austrians, Kurt Diemberger and Willi Bauer, carried on down with a Pole Drobislawa Wolf, but later that day she, too, collapsed and died on the fixed ropes. Only Diemberger and Bauer escaped alive and they had serious frostbite.*

Books have been written about that summer on K2: people want to understand what went wrong. There are many possible explanations but the simplest is that the climbers spent too long near the summit, above 8000 metres, delayed by storms in the death zone* where no one should stay for more than two days.

KANGCHENJUNGA see TREASURY OF THE FIVE SNOWS

KARABINER see CLIMBING GEAR

KARAKORAM HIGHWAY

They called it the Eighth Wonder of the World. It is one of the most remarkable roads on Earth and was built during the 1970s to encourage trade between Pakistan and China. It was so dangerous to build that it is said that for every mile of the road a worker was killed. A plaque at the side of the road reads:

> Some time in the future, when others will ply the KKH, little will they realize the amount of sweat, courage,

> dedication, endurance and human sacrifice that has gone into the making of this road; but as you drive along, tarry a little to say a short prayer for those silent brave men of the Pakistan army, who gave their lives to realize a dream now known as the Karakoram Highway.

Hundreds of thousands of tonnes of dynamite were used to blast a way through the greatest mountains on this planet. Before, there was just a narrow jeep track; now large buses and trucks can travel at speed.

The Karakoram Highway starts from Pakistan's capital, Islamabad. It crosses some fairly low mountains to the Indus river. From there it climbs, winding its way up the mighty Indus valley to the town of Gilgit. North of Gilgit it enters the famous Hunza* valley. Finally, after a journey of 873 kilometres from Islamabad, it crosses the Kunjerab pass at 4934 metres and enters Chinese Sinkiang. From there it runs through high desert country to the city of Kashgar. From Kashgar it is possible to continue by road all the way to Beijing. In fact you can now drive all the way from Karachi, Pakistan's southern sea port, to Peking, a journey of 7250 kilometres.

During a journey up the Karakoram Highway you nearly always have to stop at some point and wait for a landslide to be cleared. The Karakoram mountains are part of the Greater Himalaya* range, one of the youngest mountain ranges on Earth and therefore still unstable. The Pakistan army works night and day to keep the road open.

KILIMANJARO

In Africa, 200 miles south of the equator, elephants, antelopes and giraffe graze in the national parks of Kenya and Tanzania. High above them snow seems to float in the sky, the eternal snow of Kilimanjaro, the highest mountain in Africa.

Kilimanjaro is an extinct volcano. The summit crater no longer spews flame into the air; it lies quiet under a cloak of snow and ice. Glaciers* slide, like spilt ice cream, down the sides of the mountain.

Every year thousands of people climb Kilimanjaro. Some climb the difficult routes on the west side of the mountain, but most follow the easier route from the east.

The climb from the east takes four days. First you walk through thick forest, where you might see elephants. Then comes a forest of giant heathers growing up to 15 metres high, then open meadows with extraordinary giant lobelias, looking like plants from another planet, leading into a long plod across a great bare stony plain to the final hut.

The last day is very hard. You leave in the cold dark hours before dawn. A local guide shows you the way up a steep scree* slope. Eventually there is a magical moment as the sun rises over the great plain of Africa, far below. Most people stop on the rim of the crater at Gillman's Point but some find the energy to climb the last 200 metres to the highest point, Uhuru Peak, 5895 metres above sea level. The air is thin* and many feel weak on this final stretch.

LAMA

In 1922 the first British Everest Expedition arrived at Rongbuk monastery, in a remote valley of Tibet,* below the world's highest summit. Before setting foot on the dangerous mountain the climbers were blessed by the head lama.

A lama is a monk who spends his life studying the teachings of the Buddha. Buddhism is the religion of several Himalayan countries, Tibet, Bhutan, parts of Nepal, and Ladakh in northern India. Until recently every family would send one boy to become a lama. In Tibet there were tens of thousands of lamas and the country was ruled by a chief lama, called the Dalai Lama. Then in 1950 the Chinese army invaded Tibet and the Dalai Lama fled across the Himalaya* to India, where he still lives in exile. In Tibet hundreds of monasteries were destroyed and now only a few remain.

Many Tibetans now travel to Nepal and India to train as lamas in the monasteries there. They all wear the same uniform of dark red and orange robes and shave their heads. During religious services they chant prayers in low voices, accompanied by drums, cymbals, horns, oboes and bells.

LEMON MOUNTAINS

Percy Lemon was a scientist who, whilst flying over the east coast of Greenland in the early 1930s, discovered what are now called the Lemon Mountains. They are just one of the many mountain ranges along the coast of Greenland and there are only two ways to get to them: you can approach by boat, but even in summer icebergs are often floating around the coast, and sometimes the ice is so thick that boats cannot get through; or the easier way is to land by plane on the ice cap, behind the mountains. The ice cap is an immense glacier,* a great sheet of ice that lies across the centre of Greenland, 3000 metres above sea level. It is as big as the whole of France and Germany combined.

LENIN

During the nineteenth century Russia built up a vast empire, stretching far into Central Asia. In a distant corner of this empire, squeezed between China and Afghanistan, lies a range of mountains called the Pamirs. One of these great snowy peaks is called Pik Lenina. The summit is 7134 metres above sea level and is the second highest in the range. It was named after Lenin, who in 1917 led the Russian Revolution.

The highest peak (7483 metres) was named Pik Stalin after Lenin's successor. Later, when the Russian people realized what an evil ruler Stalin had been, they renamed the mountain 'Peak of Communism'. Now that the Communist USSR has collapsed and Pik Communism is in the newly independent state of Tadzhikstan, perhaps the Tadzhiks will change its name again.

LITTER

Many of the extinct volcanoes* in Chile and Peru were unclimbed until the twentieth century – at least, that is what people thought, until they discovered the remains of shelters and shrines hundreds of years old on the summits. Archaeologists believe they were left by South America Indians who climbed the peaks to make sacrifices during the fifteenth century.

The summit remains in South America are some of the oldest mountain litter. Nowadays more and more mountains show signs of human activity. Many famous climbs in the Himalaya* are littered with old fixed ropes, half-destroyed tents and discarded gas cylinders. On mountains everywhere, climbers leave behind pitons and nuts, used as anchors for abseiling.*

Most people do not mind finding the odd piece of metal in the mountains and the occasional sign that someone else has been there before can be quite comforting. However, if there are great piles of old tins, plastic packaging, used batteries and abandoned equipment, the mess can ruin what should be a beautiful wilderness. The problem arises because mountaineers are prepared to carry up all their special supplies, but too lazy, or often too exhausted, to remove everything on the way down.

High on a difficult peak the litter affects only a few mountaineers, but in the valleys it can spoil many people's pleasure. The answer is simple: only take with you things that are strictly necessary. Allow plenty of time to burn and crush all degradable litter and bury it in deep holes. Anything likely to pollute, like used batteries, should be carried down to the nearest disposal site.

LLAMA

Llama is pronounced 'yama'. It is the Spanish word for a woolly animal that roams around the Andes mountains in Peru, Bolivia and Ecuador. The llama looks rather like a sheep, but with long legs and a very long neck. It is, in fact, related to the camel and, like the camel, it looks disapprovingly down its nose at strangers.

Instead of a hoof each foot has a leather pad, like a slipper, with two thick claws for climbing steep mountainsides.

The llama is a domestic animal, bred by the Inca* people from its wild relations like the vicuna. The llama is still used as a pack animal to carry luggage along steep mountain paths. Loading up a llama takes a lot of skill and patience: the animal often loses its temper, spitting half-eaten food in the owner's face.

If you visit the Andes* you will also see alpacas. They are similar to llamas but are bred especially for their thick soft wool.

GEORGE MALLORY

George Mallory wanted desperately to be the first person to climb Everest.* Three times, in 1921, 1922 and 1924, he left his wife and children to sail to India, travel up into Tibet* and spend weeks on the bleak windy Rongbuk glacier.* By the third attempt he had had enough of these long absences from home. He wrote to his wife saying that he hoped that this time he would be successful and not have to return again to Tibet. On 8 June 1924 he set off with Sandy Irvine from camp VI, high on the North Ridge of Everest, hoping to get to the summit that day. Later that morning another climber, Noel Odell, watching from lower down, saw two tiny figures edging towards the summit. They still had a long way to go and were moving very slowly. After a few minutes, clouds drifted across the mountain, hiding the two figures. They were never seen again.

It is just possible that Mallory and Irvine reached the summit of Everest in 1924 but most experts think it unlikely. However, Mallory's name will always be associated with Everest, and with a famous quotation. A short time before he died, Mallory was lecturing in America. He grew tired of the endless questions and when asked for the hundredth time why he wanted to climb Everest, he said, 'Because it's there.'

MARCO POLO'S SHEEP

Over seven hundred years ago the Italian adventurer Marco Polo walked all the way from Venice to China. His journey east took him through Afghanistan, across the Oxus river and up into the high mountains called the Pamirs. He met the nomads who wander across the great open grasslands of the Pamirs and he heard about huge wild sheep with immense horns. When he returned to Europe in 1273 he wrote about them in his journal. Nearly six hundred years passed before Europeans again visited the mountains of Central Asia and saw the sheep which Marco Polo had described. They named them Marco Polo sheep.

An adult Marco Polo sheep stands 1.3 metres tall at the shoulders. The male has horns up to 2 metres long that curve round almost in complete circles.

Since Marco Polo's time the sheep's numbers have declined. In winter they often get bogged down in snowdrifts or wiped out by avalanches.* They fall prey to wolves and snow leopards,* but their most dangerous enemies are human hunters. In the Pamirs and other parts of Central Asia, Marco Polo horns litter the ground everywhere: the nomads use them to make fences round their camps, or carve them into bowls. They say that sometimes foxes shelter in the hollowed remains of the biggest ones.

MARMOT

An eagle's shadow flits across the Alpine meadow. A large furry rodent stands up on its hind legs, eyes alert with fear, and lets out a piercing whistle. His friends take the warning and in seconds they are all scurrying across the hillside, heading for large stony burrows. One last look round and they scamper underground.

The marmot is a ground squirrel. It lives in the high mountain meadows of Europe, America and Asia. All winter it hibernates underground and in Alaska a species of marmot sleeps for nine months of the year! For a few weeks during the summer the marmots come out to feed on the Alpine flowers and grasses and their whistle is a common sound.

The European marmot is the size of a large rabbit. There are bigger ones in Asia and a close relation called the prairie dog in North America.

MATTERHORN

Edward Whymper never meant to be a mountaineer – he was a professional artist and he first came to the Alps* in 1860 to make illustrations for a journal called *Peaks, Passes and Glaciers* – but when he first saw the Matterhorn, he knew that he had to climb it.

Edward Whymper

The Matterhorn is one of the world's most beautiful mountains. It is a massive four-sided pyramid that stands all alone, towering above the Swiss valley of Zermatt to the north and the Italian valley of Cervinia to the south. It was an Italian, Jean-Anthoine Carrel, who first dared to try to climb the mountain, at the same time that Whymper came to Zermatt. The following year Whymper returned to make his own attempt. The race was on.

Carrel, Whymper and another Englishman called Tyndall tried again and again to find a way to the top of the Matterhorn. Then, in 1865, Whymper and his Swiss guides attempted a different route – the North-East Ridge, which soars up directly above Zermatt. From the valley this ridge looks impossible, but once they were on it the climbers discovered that, for most of the way, the angle is quite gentle.

The Matterhorn had become so famous that many climbers were competing to make the first ascent. On this particular day seven people started up the North-East Ridge. That night they bivouacked* high on the ridge. The next day they continued up much steeper slopes, where they had to move very carefully on the frozen north side of the ridge. But the weather remained fine and, as Whymper recorded, 'At 1.40 p.m. the world was at our feet and the Matterhorn was conquered.' Three hundred metres lower down, Carrel and his Italian companions were still toiling up the South-West Ridge. To make things even worse for the Italians, Whymper started rolling boulders down towards them, proving that the British can be as unsporting as anyone.

The British triumph was short-lived. As so often happens, an accident marred the descent. The British party was roped together: the French guide, Michel Croz, went first, followed by the inexperienced nineteen-year-old Douglas Hadow. Above Hadow were his friend the Reverend George Hudson and Lord Francis Douglas. Soon after the party left the summit, young Hadow slipped and knocked off Croz. They fell, pulling off Hudson and Douglas. Above them, Whymper and the two remaining climbers, the Taugwalders, clung desperately to the rocks. The rope jerked tight on Peter Taugwalder, who kept his stance. But at the same instant there was a sound which Whymper would remember all his life – the snapping of the rope.

Whymper and the Taugwalders watched helplessly as their four companions slid, bounced and cartwheeled down the North Face, gathering speed then disappearing over a 1200-metre drop to plunge to their certain deaths. Badly shaken, the survivors slowly continued their own descent, only reaching Zermatt the following day.

Modern nylon ropes are much stronger than the hemp ropes used in 1865. Even so, people still make mistakes and have accidents on the Matterhorn. Sometimes helicopters have to retrieve bodies from the mountain and the Zermatt graveyard is full of Matterhorn victims. But many thousands have now returned safely from the summit. On a busy summer day three or four hundred people may reach it and most still take the route pioneered by Whymper and his guides. In spite of the crowds, the Matterhorn remains

an inspiring mountain. Its unique shape has appeared on countless calendars, cards, jigsaws, chocolate wrappers and muesli boxes; it is probably the most photographed mountain in the world.

REINHOLD MESSNER

Reinhold was woken at five o'clock. He crawled out of the warm hay, pushed back the heavy barn door, saw the frosty stars and put on his clothes. Half an hour later he set off through the forest with his father, mother and brother. They climbed up through the meadows, then on up steep scree* slopes until at last the real climbing began – a great rock gully* leading up through the cliffs.

Later that morning Reinhold Messner stood on his first summit. It was 1949 and he was just five years old. Already he was fascinated by the Dolomite mountains – range after range of them, filling the horizons around his home in northern Italy. With his brothers he spent every spare moment wandering in them. Soon the boys started to try difficult climbs and by the time they left school they were completing some of the most taxing ones in the Dolomites.

Messner later lost two of his brothers in mountain accidents. Siegfried was killed by lightning in 1985 while Gunther had died fifteen years earlier, in an avalanche* on Nanga Parbat in the Himalaya. Reinhold and Gunther had just climbed a treacherous new route on Nanga Parbat. They descended by a different one but when they were almost safely down Gunther was snatched away by a huge ice avalanche.

It was a terrible tragedy for Reinhold. At least he was alive, but he only just survived the ordeal and suffered serious frostbite.* Back in Italy several toes had to be amputated. But he was determined to continue mountaineering – it was his life and passion. When his feet had recovered, he returned to the Himalaya. For fifteen years he returned time and again. Sometimes he was successful; sometimes he failed. At first he climbed with large expeditions, trying some of the most demanding unclimbed faces on the world's highest mountains. But then he thought, 'Why do we have to have all these people, like a great circus travelling through the mountains? Why not climb with just two?'

In 1975 Messner took the big step into the unknown, by attempting one of the world's great 8000-metre peaks as a two-person team. With the Austrian guide Peter Habeler, he climbed a new route up Hidden Peak in Pakistan. The final climb took just three days up and down. No one had seen anything like it before: no porters, no fixed ropes, no preparation, just two men, moving very fast, carrying the tiniest tent imaginable.

Everest* came next in 1978. Messner and Habeler took another big step into the unknown: they were the first to reach the summit without oxygen equipment. Even today very few people have repeated their feat.

Messner was always trying something new. Later that summer he returned to Nanga Parbat, where his brother had died, and climbed the mountain alone – the first solo ascent of an 8000-metre peak. Two years later he soloed Everest. Other climbs followed, always in the thin air* of the Himalaya. Messner realized that he could climb *all* the

fourteen 8000-metre peaks, but a Polish climber, Jerzy Kukuczka, was catching up with him. The race was on.

Messner just won. In 1986 he climbed his last two 8000-metre peaks: Makalu and Lhotse. He had come a long way from that first climb in the Dolomites.

MONT BLANC

The highest mountain in Europe is Elbruz, in the Caucasus mountains of Georgia, but the highest mountain in the Alps* is Mont Blanc: the White Mountain. Its summit is a huge dome of ice, coated thickly with snow. It gleams far above the valley of Chamonix.

Over two hundred years ago, people began to wonder if it might be possible to climb to the top of Mont Blanc. Since 1642 scientists had known that air pressure drops as you climb higher above sea level. Climbing Mont Blanc would be a way of finding out more about this change in pressure. In 1760 a scientist called Horace Benedict de Saussure offered a prize for the first people to reach the summit of the great snow peak, which finally went to two men from the village of Chamonix, who had grown up in the mountain's shadow. In 1786 Dr Michel Paccard and a crystal hunter, Jacques Balmat, found a route up great snowfields and through mazes of crevasses* and ice towers to the 4807-metre summit. Although the altitude made them short of breath, they returned safely (see THIN AIR). The next year de Saussure himself climbed Mont Blanc, later followed by other scientists. Because of the clear air at high altitude, the top of Mont Blanc was a good site for an observatory. One hut was built on the summit, but because this is formed from a moving sheet of ice, the hut soon collapsed. However, the Vallot Observatory, built in 1890, on solid rocks just below the summit, still survives, providing emergency shelter for climbers caught in blizzards.

Many routes have now been climbed up Mont Blanc. The best and hardest are on the huge precipices on the southern side. Like most great mountains, Mont Blanc forms an international frontier and this southern flank lies in Italy, where the mountain is known as Monte Bianco.

MORAINE

Glaciers* are like giant bulldozers or snowploughs, scraping and pushing mountain rubbish down to the valley. Rocks fall continually from a mountain, landing on the glacier below. As the glacier slides slowly down into the valley it takes the rocks with it. Sometimes they form dark straight lines on the surface of the ice. These stripes are called *medial* moraines.

Medial moraines form down the middle of glaciers. *Lateral* moraines form along the sides: the glacier pushes earth and boulders out to the side. These side or lateral moraines can be hundreds of metres high. On the glacier side they are dangerous cliffs of rubble, but behind the moraine there is often a beautiful little valley. These valleys make lovely campsites: they have grass, flowers, streams and sometimes trees, like a hidden garden just a few metres from the ice and rubble of the glacier.

Near their snouts some glaciers are very ugly. The surface is covered in slushy mud, gravel and boulders. It looks like a dead wasteland – a giant rubbish tip.

Over the centuries glaciers advance and retreat. Sometimes a glacier surges forward, pushing earth and boulders in front, like a pig's snout rooting in the ground. Then a few years later it may retreat, leaving behind a great heap of boulders, called a *terminal* moraine.

MOUNTAINS AS ISLANDS

Some of the world's islands are really mountain summits, the tips of volcanoes* that have risen from the bed of the ocean. One of the most famous of these volcanic islands is Hawaii, in the Pacific. Hawaii has two summits; the highest, Mauna Kea, rises

4205 metres above sea level. However, if it is measured from its real base on the bed of the ocean, it is taller than Everest.*

In 1963 a new mountain appeared out of the sea near Iceland. This young volcano, the world's newest mountain, is called Surtsey.

NANDA DEVI

Nanda Devi, the Goddess mountain of India, is guarded by a great wall of icy peaks, through which explorers longed to find a way. In 1934 the British explorers Eric Shipton and Bill Tilman found the route: a deep river gorge called the Rishi Ganga. With their local porters and some Sherpa* friends they had to edge their way, metre by metre, up the narrow gorge. Sometimes they had to climb high up the side to pass overhanging cliffs. At other times they had to cross almost vertical slopes of slippery grass. They finally found their reward when they emerged into the Sanctuary, a paradise of flower meadows and glaciers, hidden from the outside world, rising out of which was Nanda Devi, the highest mountain in India.

Two years later, in 1936, Bill Tilman returned with a group of British and American climbers. It was a happy and successful expedition. After several weeks' work, Tilman and Noel Odell reached the summit of Nanda Devi, 7817 metres above sea level. For the next sixteen years it remained the highest summit reached by man.

One of the American climbers returned to Nanda Devi forty years later to try a difficult new route. The team included a famous climber, Willi Unsoeld, and his twenty-two-year-old daughter, named Nanda Devi after one of the most beautiful mountains in the world.

It was not a happy expedition. Quarrels and the bad monsoon weather made life difficult on the mountain, but after some hard climbing two members reached the summit. A few days later a second team, including Willi and Nanda Devi Unsoeld, came up to have a go at it.

Bad weather kept them waiting at the top camp. Then Nanda Devi Unsoeld started to feel ill, so they descended to a lower camp. That night she was kept awake by bad stomach pains. In the morning the others packed up to take her down, but when they were ready she suddenly said, very calmly, 'I am going to die.' A moment later she fell unconscious. Her father tried to revive her with his own breath but after fifteen minutes he felt her lips grow cold. She was dead.

They buried her there, in the snows of Nanda Devi. The local people said that Nanda Devi Unsoeld was the goddess in human form, and had come back to live on her mountain.

NEEDLES

Some of the most exciting mountains are like slender needles pointing up into the sky. In the English Lake District there is a famous rock spire called Napes Needle, where the sport of rock climbing* is said to have been invented. At Chamonix, in France, there is a cluster of granite needles. They are called the Aiguilles de Chamonix, the Needles of Chamonix. This French word 'aiguille' is used to describe other pointed mountains around the world.

NUT see CLIMBING GEAR

OGRES

Long before people dreamed of climbing mountains they gave them names. Some mountains they worshipped; others were feared. Above the Swiss village of Grindelwald there is a famous group of three peaks – a 'triptych'. The highest, on the right, is a graceful mountain called the Jungfrau, the Young Woman. The next is called the Monch, the Monk, because it is shaped rather like the hood worn by monks. The third peak of the triptych, on the left, is a dark giant of a mountain. For much of the year it blocks out the sun's rays, keeping the village of Grindelwald in shadow. They call it the Eiger, the Ogre.

The North-West Face of the Eiger is probably the biggest mountain wall in Europe. It rises 1600 metres straight out of the meadows. At its base it is nearly a mile wide. It is like an immense shell, waiting to catch the clouds and storms that approach from the west.

In the 1930s mountaineers began to think about climbing the Eigerwand, the Ogre Wall. It was terrifying but fascinating, the greatest challenge in the European Alps.* It was a giant 'mixed' climb: there were hard rock climbing, ice climbing, snow and sometimes a mixture of all three. In bad weather it was almost impossible to get back down the wall, as the Ogre threw everything at any climber who dared to come near. Waterfalls drenched clothing and ropes, which later froze solid. Stones fell hundreds of metres, smashing the lower slopes like bullets. Avalanches* poured down the chimneys* and gullys.*

During the first attempts few climbers returned alive. In 1935 two young Austrians were nearly half-way up the wall when a terrible storm closed in. When it cleared, people could see them through the telescope, frozen dead at their bivouac.* Today that ledge is still called Death Bivouac.

The following year, 1936, four more Austrians died trying to retreat during a storm. The last to die was Toni Kurz, who was trying to lower himself on a rope to rescuers. All night long he struggled with numb fingers to untangle the frozen ropes. By morning he was only a few metres from his rescuers, dangling beneath an overhang. They could almost touch him where he hung, but after that terrible night his body could cope no more. He muttered, 'It is finished,' and slumped over, dead on the rope.

The Eigerwand was acquiring a terrible reputation, but still mountaineers came, most of whom were Germans and Austrians. At that time Germany was in the midst of a terrible depression, life was hard and jobs were scarce, so

for some young climbers the mountains were almost an escape. They loved the freedom and the adventure. The best climbers looked for the excitement of climbing new routes where no one had ever trodden before. Of all the mountain walls in the Alps, the Eigerwand was the biggest and most difficult and it was one of the last that remained unclimbed.

In 1938 two more Austrians, Heinrich Harrer and Fritz Kasparek, were half-way up the wall when two Germans, Anderl Heckmair and Wiggerl Vorg, caught up with them. The Austrians had only old-fashioned nailed boots, but the German leader, Heckmair, had modern crampons for ice climbing. As the Austrians were moving very slowly Heckmair offered generously to team up with them and lead a united team of four, using his new twelve-point crampons on the difficult ice sections.

The four men passed Death Bivouac and continued up into the unknown. They bivouacked* on 'The Ramp' then the next day discovered the vital ledge, which they called 'The Traverse of the Gods', which led eventually to the 'Exit Cracks'. By now the weather had broken and the men had to bivouac again, cramped and freezing on a tiny ledge. Vorg sat awake all night, letting the leader Heckmair lean on his back, so that he could get some sleep and save his strength for the next day.

In the morning they were lost in cloud. It was snowing. Every few minutes avalanches crashed down. Several times Heckmair was knocked off his feet. On one fall he skewered Vorg's hand with his crampons, staining the snow red with fresh blood. But he continued fighting – for his and his friends' lives. He *had* to find a way up the 'Exit Cracks'.

Heckmair succeeded; it was one of the most brilliant pieces of climbing ever achieved in the history of mountaineering. The awesome Eigerwand had finally been conquered.

Now several hundred people have climbed the Eigerwand. It has been climbed in winter; it has been soloed; there are new routes up the wall; in good weather the 1938

route can be enjoyable. But things can still go wrong. All sensible mountaineers realize that, even with modern equipment, the Eigerwand is dangerous. And they all think back with respect to Anderl Heckmair.

There is another Ogre, in Pakistan. The first ascent of that Ogre in 1977 was just as exciting. Two British climbers, Chris Bonington* and Doug Scott, reached the summit late in the afternoon. It was already dark as they started to descend. Doug Scott was abseiling* when he skidded on some ice and went into a huge swing. At the end of the swing his legs crashed against a rock wall, and both ankles were broken.

It was a desperate situation – two broken legs at 7000 metres, far from help. It took a week to get off the mountain. Doug Scott had to abseil and climb down the whole way on his knees. To make matters worse, a storm blinded the party with driving snow. Luckily two other climbers, Clive Rowland and Mo Anthoine, were at the top camp. Without their help, Bonington and Scott might never have got down.

Afterwards Bonington wrote in the *American Alpine Journal*: 'I felt that the Ogre had allowed us to climb it and then, like a great cat, had played games with us all the way down, finally allowing us to escape.'

OLYMPICS

Every four years, skiers, skaters, lugers and bob-sleighers gather to compete in the Winter Olympics. Each time a different mountain resort is chosen for the games. In 1992, it was the turn of Albertville, in the French Alps.

The 1992 Winter Olympics were as exciting as ever with the usual incredible display of speed skiing, downhill racing, slalom, ski jumping, speed skating, figure skating and a bob-sleigh run. The cost of the entertainment was immeasurable, in both ecological and financial terms.

The games were spread over fourteen different mountain resorts, which had to accommodate 2300 competitors, 7000 journalists and over a million spectators. Forests were cleared to build a new motorway. At La Plagne the specially built bob-sleigh ice run was kept cool with poisonous ammonia. At Courcheval 30,000 tonnes of concrete were pumped in to make a new ski jump. At Val d'Isère 40,000 cubic metres of earth were scraped away from the hillside to prepare the men's downhill race course. Everywhere the mountains suffered, and 2600 square kilometres of alpine forests and meadows were carved up to create the various events. Many people were angered by the ecological damage caused by the 1992 Winter Olympics. In future, any country offering to host the games may have to present a plan, showing how it is going to limit such ecological damage.

Mountaineering is not an Olympic sport, but occasionally mountaineers have been given special Olympic medals for achievement. In 1930 the brothers Toni and Franz Smidt received an award for making the first ascent of the Matterhorn North Face. In 1988 Reinhold Messner* and Jerzy Kukuczka were offered Olympic medals for being the first people to climb all the world's 8000-metre peaks.

By the year 2000 there will probably be an Olympic climbing event. Some of the world's best rock climbers now compete on artificial climbing walls and these competitions may eventually be included in the Olympic Games.

OXYGEN see THIN AIR

PARAGLIDERS

Icarus tried to fly: in the ancient Greek myth, he made wings out of feathers, but he flew too high, too close to the sun, and the wax holding his wings together melted. He plummeted to his death. We now know much more about the mechanics of flying and also

that as you climb into the atmosphere the air gets colder, not hotter.

The hang glider is like a miniature plane with a simple frame of light metal tubing, but simplest of all is the 'paraglider', half parachute, half glider. You sit in a harness, suspended by thin lines from a large nylon sail. To take off you run down a slope, into the wind, filling the sail with air until it lifts your body off the ground. With skill you can steer the paraglider accurately, travelling long distances as you slowly descend to earth.

Paragliders are now a common sight in the mountains, like huge brilliant coloured birds soaring in the sky. A paraglider weighs only a few kilograms and can be folded easily away inside rucksacks. Some mountaineers carry them up climbs. If the wind is right when they reach the summit they just jump off and fly back down to the valley.

It looks easy, but paragliding can be dangerous. Everything depends on the wind,* which, in the mountains, can be unpredictable.

PASS see also COL

A mountain pass is a gap; it is a way through the mountains. Even so, you usually have to climb a long way to reach a pass and many passes are only open in summer: in winter it is too difficult to keep clearing the snowdrifts.

Many famous passes have been known for centuries: the Khyber pass in Afghanistan, the Athabasca pass in Canada, the Llanberis pass in Wales, and the high Alpine passes that linked northern Europe to Italy. In 218 BC Hannibal the Great crossed one of these Alpine passes with elephants. He had come all the way from Africa, up through Spain and France, and wanted to take Rome by surprise, frightening the Roman armies with his elephants. Before he could march down through Italy he had first to cross the Alps, asking local guides to show him the way across one of the high passes. His plan succeeded, but only just, after a hard struggle through the mountains.

Nowadays the big Alpine passes have tarmac roads, which climb up in a series of sharp zig-zags, although bridges and tunnels have straightened out some of the bends. Where there is a risk of avalanches* the road is usually protected by a concrete roof. In spite of all this engineering, some of the highest passes are still open for only five months a year.

One of the highest trails in the world is the Karakoram pass. There is no motor road, but for centuries travellers took horses along this route going north from India to the great markets of the Silk Road in Sinkiang. The Karakoram is really a series of passes, each higher than the last, crossing some of the most desolate country in the world. Over the years many packhorses have died from hunger, cold and exhaustion. Today their bones still litter the trail.

Since the 1950s few travellers have crossed the Karakoram pass. However, another pass further west – the Khunjerab pass – is crossed by the Karakoram Highway. It is a proper road pass and every day trucks and buses cross over between Pakistan and China.

PATAGONIA

Patagonia lies at the southern tip of the Andes,* in South America. The land is divided between Chile and Argentina, but the area is still known as Patagonia.

It is a wild and beautiful place, but its climate is harsh because it lies in the path of the southern winds that blast out of the Pacific ocean. The Pacific coast of Patagonia is split by hundreds of creeks, channels and islands. Glaciers* flow right down to the sea and between them the hills are covered in thick forest. Further inland, above the forests, there is a huge ice cap, and rising out of it are some of the most spectacular mountains on earth, steep towers of granite, like Fitzroy, Cerro Torre and the Towers of Paine.

On the east side of Patagonia lies the pampas, an area of rolling grasslands where the farmers keep huge herds of cattle and sheep. It is wonderful country for horse riding. In the wilder areas you sometimes see guanaco, a type of wild llama.* Condors,* the greatest birds of prey on Earth, soar in the sky overhead.

PHOTOGRAPHERS

Everyone was amazed when the Slovenian mountaineer Tomo Cesen came back from Nepal in 1990, saying that he had just climbed the South Face of Lhotse. Lhotse is the fourth highest mountain in the world. For years, teams of the world's best mountaineers had been trying to climb its immense south face, a huge precipice nearly 4000 metres high. Now Cesen had done it alone, in just three days.

It was one of the most brilliant climbs ever achieved, and Tomo Cesen's picture appeared on his nation's postage stamps. All the mountaineering magazines published the story of his amazing climb. It was only after a few months had gone by that some climbers started to express doubts. Normally a mountaineer's word is trusted, but people usually take photographs of important climbs as proof that they have done them.

Tomo Cesen's account of his climb was a little vague; and he had no pictures of the summit. Although most other mountaineers believed him, some thought he never reached it. And because he had no photographs of himself on the summit, he had no way of proving that he had been there.

Most people who visit mountains like to take photographs, anyway, for their own enjoyment. Occasionally, a particularly brilliant mountain photographer emerges. One of the most famous of all was the Italian Vittorio Sella. He went on many expeditions led by the Duke of Abruzzi, including the 1909 expedition to K2.* He took with him a huge plate camera weighing many kilograms, but it was worth the effort because his photographs of K2 and the surrounding mountains are some of the best that have ever been taken.

America has produced some excellent mountain photographers. Ansel Adams, who was taking photographs through most of the early years of this century, used a large plate camera to make his incredible black and white pictures of the cliffs of Yosemite. Bradford Washburn specialized in aerial photography, taking thousands of pictures of Mount McKinley and other famous Alaskan peaks. He used an aerial camera weighing 20 kilograms, which he had to hold on his lap, as he sat on a chair leaning out of the aircraft doorway. Washburn, the chair and the camera all had to be tied on for safety! Many of Washburn's aerial photographs were used to make mountain maps. In 1988 he achieved his life's ambition by arranging special flights over Everest.* The pictures were stunning and the final result was an accurate new map of the world's highest mountain.

Satellite photographs, taken from space, can also be useful for mapping mountains. However, they do not show everything. Above a certain altitude the mountains are covered in permanent snow and on satellite photographs this snowy area tends to come out blank white with no detail. In spite of all the technology now available, there are still, high in the world's most remote mountains, some little 'blanks on the map'.*

PITON see CLIMBING GEAR

PLANT HUNTERS

They were bunched together in a narrow valley, all eighty of them, when the Tibetans attacked. Sixty-eight people were killed on the spot. The survivors fled through the mountain gorges of Yunnan, in south-west China. Among those who fled was a Scotsman, George Forrest. For two days he was followed by enemy scouts. Eventually he threw away his boots to make his tracks less clear, but the scouts still kept up with him. At one point he hid up to his neck in an icy river, but he was spotted and only escaped death by a miracle when two poisoned arrows shot through the top of his hat, skimming within millimetres of his scalp.

Forrest managed to escape again, but still his enemies pursued him. For another six days he struggled through bamboo thickets, across glaciers* and over bare rocks that tore his feet to ribbons. Eventually he reached a farm where he thought he was safe, but on the edge of a field he stepped on a booby trap, a sharpened bamboo stake that passed right between the bones of his foot and out through the top.

In agony he tore his bleeding foot free and hobbled on, half dead, until finally he stumbled into a French missionary centre protected by Chinese troops. At last he was safe.

That terrible massacre happened in 1905. The previous year a British expedition had crossed the Himalaya* from India and invaded Tibet. Suddenly Europeans, 'white devils', became very unpopular with the Tibetans, who also had a dispute with China, and all Europeans in neighbouring Yunnan were attacked viciously.

In spite of his terrifying experience, George Forrest returned many times to Yunnan. He was neither a soldier, a politician nor a missionary. He was one of many great explorers who took risks and suffered hardships, travelling for years through the mountains of Asia in search of green treasure: plants.

Many of the flowers and shrubs that we see in western

gardens were introduced from Asia. One of the first great plant hunters was the director of Kew Gardens, in London, another Scot, called Joseph Hooker. During 1848 and 1849 he explored the Himalayan kingdoms of Sikkim and Nepal, collecting thousands of dried plant specimens and seeds to send back to Kew. He was the first European to get anywhere near the great peaks of Kangchenjunga, but he is best remembered for the beautiful great flowering rhododendron trees that he introduced from the slopes of the Himalaya.

There were many other famous plant hunters: a French missionary, Armand David, collected hundreds of thousands of seeds from the mountains of Yunnan. The Scottish botanist William Douglas introduced the Douglas fir from the Rocky mountains of Canada. Frank Kingdon Ward spent nearly every year between 1909 and 1956 travelling through the unknown mountains of Tibet, China and Burma, bringing back countless plant specimens, from the seeds of great magnolia trees to the most delicate primulas.

Perhaps the most remarkable of all was Ernest Wilson. In 1903 he discovered the Regal Lily (*Regule*) in the Chinese province of Szechuan. Seven years later he returned to collect bulbs for an American arboretum. Everything went fine until Wilson was on his way back, with his porters carrying 7000 lily bulbs along a dangerous mountain track. Suddenly a boulder crashed down the hillside and knocked Wilson to the ground, snapping his leg in two places. Despite the agony, he managed to stay calm and splint his crushed leg with a camera tripod. But then he saw a caravan of fifty mules heading towards him. The track was too narrow for the mules to turn round, so Wilson told the porters to place him carefully across the track. For the next ten terrifying minutes he lay there, dead still, while each of the fifty mules stepped across his battered leg.

Wilson's leg became badly infected and for the rest of his life it was shorter than the other. However, he thought that

his 'lily limp' was a price worth paying. Now gardeners all over the world thank the botanist who brought back one of the most beautiful and sweet-smelling of all lilies from the wild mountains of Szechuan.

POLAND

On 17 February 1980, two Polish mountaineers, Leszek Cichy and Krzysztof Wielicki, stood on the summit of Everest,* the first people ever to reach the top of the world in winter. Climbing the world's highest peaks at that time of year is a tough game and so far only the Poles have had much success at it.

Poland has had a hard history: the country was invaded repeatedly by Russia and Germany, its economy was wrecked and it is still a poor nation compared with, say, Britain or America or Australia. But in spite of this Poland has always had a proud national spirit, which perhaps has helped Polish mountaineers to achieve so much success.

Also, during the years of Communist rule it was very hard for Poles to leave their country, but a few mountaineers were allowed to travel to the Himalaya.* If they were successful there was more chance of getting permission and money for further expeditions abroad. The only mountains in Poland are the Tatras, on the border with Czechoslovakia. They are beautiful, rather like the Alps,* with very cold winters. For the most dedicated Polish mountaineers, winter climbs in the Tatras are a good training for the Himalaya.

Poland has produced many of the world's top Himalayan mountaineers, including Wanda Rutkiewicz, the first woman to climb K2.*

POPOCATAPETL

In 1519 the Spanish *conquistador* Hernan Cortès conquered the Aztec empire of Mexico with a force of just 500 men. From Mexico City he noticed a plume of smoke rising from a high mountain. A group of the *conquistadores* went to investigate, but as they climbed up the lower slopes a shower of ashes rained down, driving them off the mountain. Three years later Francisco Montano made the first recorded ascent of the 5452-metre-high volcano,* Popocatapetl. From the summit rim Montano was lowered on a rope into the fiery pit of the crater, where he collected 300 pounds of sulphur to be sent back to Spain. However, the Spanish authorities decided that it was easier to mine sulphur in their own country. Popocatapetl is dormant and now sleeps peacefully. The crater is cold and quiet and every year hundreds of people climb to the top of Mexico's highest peak.

PORTALEDGE

One of the most uncomfortable nights I ever spent was on a Himalayan climb with Dick Renshaw, another British climber. That night we had to try to sleep sitting on a narrow snow ledge, with our backs leaning against the rock wall behind and our feet resting in rope loops. If we had had Portaledges we would have had a much better night's sleep.

The Portaledge is a movable bedroom, a ledge that you fold up during the day and haul behind you in a sack. It was invented for the great overhanging rock walls of El Capitan,* in Yosemite, where there are often no natural ledges. The first climbers to attempt these great walls used to bivouac* in hammocks. But in a hammock you cannot lie flat and may be rather tightly squeezed.

A Portaledge is composed of a metal frame supporting a nylon base. When it is assembled it makes a firm flat bed. It is held up by ropes from each corner, connected to a karabiner, which is clipped into a safe anchor on the wall. For cold conditions a canopy fits over the Portaledge, making a perfect snug home that can be taken up the steepest, smoothest mountain walls.

PORTERS

In Europe, America or New Zealand you can usually get quite close to the mountains by road or railway, but in some parts of the world they still lie far from any road or city. An expedition may have to take supplies for several weeks: food, fuel, tents, climbing equipment . . . For each person there may be 200 kilograms or more of supplies – far more than he can carry himself – so help is needed to transport everything to base camp.

Expeditions to the Andes usually hire pack animals. In the Himalaya the carrying is normally done by humans: porters. Because there are no roads, the local people are used to carrying loads on their backs. In some countries, like Nepal, many people work full time as porters, carrying enormous weights. It is a hard life.

The porters who work for expeditions are sometimes farmers who want to earn some extra cash, and the mountaineers, trekkers, photographers and scientists who come from abroad can pay them much more than they normally earn. But it is still hard work. Often the porters have no proper shoes. At night they eat only the most basic food and sleep huddled under thin blankets. By day they carry loads up to 30 kilograms, usually secured with a rope across the shoulders or a headstrap around the forehead: few porters have rucksacks. In most countries only men work as porters, but in Nepal and Tibet women also carry loads.

PUNCAK JAYA

The Dutch sailor Jan Carstenz was thousands of miles from home, sailing through the East Indies. One morning he noticed a particularly bright cloud in the distance, then realized that it was not a cloud, but snow. Back in Holland people would not believe him. How could there be snow in the tropics, almost on the equator? But he was right. There *was* snow because it lay on the top of a high mountain, 4877 metres above sea level.

The mountain is on a huge island which the Dutch called New

Guinea. They named the mountain Carstenz Pyramid after the first white man to see it. Now the island of New Guinea is divided in two. The eastern part is Papua New Guinea; the western part where the mountain lies is called Irian Jaya. The people of Irian Jaya now call the mountain Puncak Jaya.

Many geographers include New Guinea with New Zealand and Australia in the continent of 'Australasia'. This makes Puncak Jaya, and not Australia's Kosciusko, the highest point in Australasia; some people trying to climb the seven highest continental summits make a special effort to visit Irian Jaya. It used to take many days of trekking through the jungle to reach Puncak Jaya, but now you can get quite close by road and cable car. The cable car was not built for tourists but for miners: near Puncak Jaya is a mountain made of solid copper ore, which is being cut away, tonne by tonne, the biggest copper mine in the world.

PUNDITS

Colonel Montgomerie longed to know what lay beyond the Himalaya,* in the distant land of Tibet. In 1863 he was in charge of the Survey of India and he wanted to explore all the area to the north of India. But Tibet was forbidden to foreigners and no white person would stand a chance of getting in unnoticed.

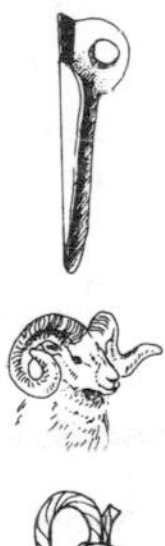

Montgomerie suddenly had an idea: Indian surveyors might be able to enter Tibet. At least their skin was the right colour and with clever disguise they might pass as Tibetan pilgrims.

For a whole year Montgomerie trained his surveyors. By the time they set off they could walk with an exact unvarying pace. By counting their paces they could measure distances for mile after mile. To keep track of all the paces they counted off the hundreds on the beads of a rosary. A rosary is a sort of necklace, worn by Tibetan pilgrims. As

well as the necklaces, Montgomerie's disguised surveyors carried other pilgrim belongings. Inside prayer wheels they hid compasses and slips of paper for taking notes. In their pilgrim's hollow staves they hid thermometers for measuring the boiling point of water. That way they could record the altitude at different points on their journeys.

With these simple instruments the surveyors collected masses of information. Sometimes they disappeared for years at a time, walking hundreds of miles through wild mountain country. They knew that if they were discovered in Tibet they could be imprisoned or even executed. The secret surveyors enabled Montgomerie to start mapping the northern side of the Himalaya and he was very proud of his unknown heroes, whom he called the Pundits.

RAILWAYS

Trains cannot climb steeply uphill, so engineers building railways through mountainous country have to find ways of laying the tracks at a gentle angle. In Peru a railway climbs through the Andes to Cuzco. To keep the angle low, the railway zig-zags, with a siding at each sharp bend so that the train can change direction each time.

Some of the best mountain railways are in the Swiss Alps.* Instead of zig-zagging backwards and forwards, the trains climb gradually in continuous spirals, winding their way in and out of tunnels and across bridges.

The Swiss have also built miniature railways called rack railways that climb much more steeply. The rack is a line of serrated steel, like a giant-toothed zip, which lies between the two rails. Underneath the train engine are special cog wheels which grip the rack, preventing the train from sliding down out of control.

The most famous rack railway in Switzerland was completed in 1912 after many years' work. It climbs right up inside the Eiger,* through a tunnel carved out of solid limestone. It starts from Grindelwald at 1000 metres; at 2320 metres it enters a tunnel at the foot of the famous Eigerwand. Higher up, tourists can get out at

Eigerwand station, inside the mountain. A short side tunnel takes them to a window where they can look out, straight down the sheer face of the Eigerwand. Occasionally they even see a climber going past.

The railway leads eventually to the Jungfraujoch. *Joch* means pass* and this high mountain pass is at 3454 metres, immediately beneath the peak of the Jungfrau – the Young Woman. It is a place for tourists to look down on the huge snowfields of the Aletsch glacier, the biggest glacier* in the Alps. For mountaineers and skiers, the Jungfraujoch railway is an easy but expensive way of getting to the heart of the mountains to start a climb or tour.

There are other famous rack railways around the world: in 1896 Welsh engineers completed a rack railway right to the top of Snowdon – to this day the carriages are still pulled by miniature steam engines – but perhaps the most famous of all miniature railways is the 'toy train' to Darjeeling, in north-east India. It was built by the British when they ruled India and it climbs up through the forest and tea plantations to the hill station of Darjeeling. From there travellers can see the distant 'Five Treasuries of the Snows', the summits of Kangchenjunga, the world's third highest mountain.

RATIONS

On expeditions mountaineers constantly talk about food. Two friends and I once spent a day sitting in a snow cave* at 7000 metres above sea level, discussing all our favourite recipes. Outside the cave a storm was raging and we had to wait five days for it to blow itself out. We had enough food to survive but we still felt hungry all the time, because we had to eke out our rations to last out the storm.

On another occasion, in India in 1992, when we had to wait four days for a helicopter to rescue me after I had broken both my legs in an accident, we ran out of food completely. On the last day we re-used the final tea bag about ten times, squeezing out every last tiny drop of flavour. The only solid food left was one boiled sweet each.

Those were unusual cases. Normally we do not run out of food because we take a lot of trouble over rations. The best mountain rations never taste as good as home food, but we try to make them as good as possible. At base camp, we eat large cooked meals, trying to build up strength for the climb. When we are on the mountain it is different: we have to carry everything on our backs, so rations have to be kept to an absolute minimum.

Each mountaineer has favourite rations for a climb, but it is important to carry food that provides plenty of energy: things like bread, butter, dried potato, noodles, cheese, salami, biscuits, chocolate, marzipan, dried fruit, sugar and dried milk. Food containing a lot of water, like fresh vegetables or fruit or anything perishable, is unsuitable because you waste energy carrying unnecessary weight. It is also silly to carry food that needs much cooking, because that means carrying more fuel for the stove. On a cold high bivouac* the easiest hot meals to prepare are things like soup, instant noodles, tea and coffee. The only cooking required is to melt snow and heat the resulting water. All that liquid is important to avoid high-altitude dehydration.*

RAVEN

One of the commonest sounds in high mountain country is the throaty croak of the raven. The raven is a very large crow, black all over, with a thick black beak and wedge-shaped tail.

Ravens live in pairs, nesting on cliff ledges. They are carrion birds, scavengers, who search for scraps and leftovers or steal eggs and young from smaller birds. They always search out mountaineers, watching and waiting for a chance to steal. They can easily rip open cardboard boxes and help themselves to the food inside.

People often confuse the raven with another black mountain bird, the chough (pronounced chuff), but the latter is very different: it is much smaller, the size of a jackdaw, and has a pointed beak. There are different species of chough, but they all have either orange or red beaks and feet.

RESCUE see HELICOPTER, OGRES, TROLL WALL

ROCK CLIMBING

High on the slopes of Great Gable, in the English Lake District, is a spire of rock called Napes Needle. In 1886 Walter Haskett-Smith found a way up it and stood precariously on its tiny summit, perched above a drop of 30 metres. It was one of the first recorded rock climbs.

Nowadays there are hundreds of thousands of rock climbers all round the world. Some cliffs are so popular that there are many routes up them. The routes are marked in guidebooks, with grades to show how difficult they are. Modern equipment means that most routes can be climbed quite safely, provided the climbers know what they are doing. On their feet they wear tight-fitting boots or shoes, with smooth soles of high friction rubber.

For a mountaineer one of the most exciting things is to find good rock climbing high on an unclimbed peak. However, many of the best rock climbers are not interested in high mountains. They prefer to concentrate on the pure challenge of extreme rock climbing. Some of the hardest routes are only 20 metres high and it takes days of practice before a climber can get all the way up without falling off.

Many of the best rock climbers now compete internationally on artificial indoor climbing walls. They are like Olympic athletes, training hard every day, building up strength and stamina so that they can hang on to the tiniest holds on fiercely overhanging walls. Because the competitions happen indoors, they make good television entertainment; but most climbers still prefer to be somewhere peaceful, out of doors, on a mountain or a sea cliff, enjoying the feeling of space beneath their feet.

ROPE see CLIMBING GEAR

RUCKSACK see CLIMBING GEAR

SALT

Salt is essential to life, yet most of us take it for granted. We buy it in packets from the shops. In parts of northern India, far from the sea, however, before the building of roads and railways there was no salt. Until the 1950s traders carried rock salt across the Himalaya* from Tibet each summer, exchanging it for rice, sugar and tea which grow only in the lowlands. They had to cross difficult passes, often walking over glaciers* 5000 metres high. The salt was often carried by sheep and goats in miniature backpacks.

SCREE

Scree is mountain rubbish, the great piles of smashed rocks that litter the slopes below cliffs. Sometimes scree slopes are several hundred metres high. If the pieces of rock are small, climbing is difficult, because every time you take a step forward you seem to slide two steps back. However, descending scree can be great fun, almost as good as skiing. The trick is to stay upright, in balance, with heels dug in, as you run and slide down the moving slope of stones. 'Scree-running' used to be popular in the English Lake District, but over the years it caused serious erosion,* so now people are encouraged to stick to the paths.

SEVEN SUMMITS

In 1984 the American Dick Bass became the first person to reach all the 'Seven Summits', the highest summit on each of the seven continents. Everest (8848 metres)* is the highest peak in Asia; Elbrus (5633 metres), in the Caucasus range, is the highest in Europe. Elbrus is an extinct volcano, as is Kilimanjaro (5895 metres), the highest mountain in Africa. In the Andes,* Aconcagua (6960 metres)* is the highest South American summit; Denali or Mount McKinley (6194 metres) is the highest in North America. The highest peak in Antarctica is Mount Vinson (5139 metres).

The seventh and easiest peak is Mount Kosciusko (2330 metres), the highest point in Australia. However, many people include Irian Jaya in a greater continent of Australasia. If this is correct, then the remote peak of Puncak Jaya (5029 metres)* is the highest summit in the Australian continent and therefore the Canadian, Pat Morrow, who climbed it in 1986 was the first.

SHERPA

In 1953 when Sherpa Tenzing Norgay* stood on the summit of Mount Everest with Edmund Hillary, his achievement made the name Sherpa famous throughout the world. The Sherpas are the 'people of the East'. They came originally from the far east of Tibet. They look like Tibetans, with black hair and slanting Mongoloid eyes. About four hundred years ago, they migrated to central Tibet,* then crossed the Himalaya*, to settle in the high valleys just south of Everest,* in a region of Nepal called Sola Khumbu.

For a long time the Sherpas remained isolated in their mountain homeland, where no foreigners were allowed. Most of them were farmers, growing small crops of barley, potatoes and vegetables and tending their yaks.* When they needed new breeding yaks, they travelled across the high Nangpa La pass to Tibet. Salt, another necessity, also came from Tibet.

Living at about 4000 metres, travelling everywhere on foot, carrying all their luggage on their backs, the Sherpas were naturally fit. When the first foreign expeditions came to the Himalaya in the 1920s, the Sherpas offered their services. Because Nepal was closed to foreigners, they had to travel to Darjeeling, in India. Many Sherpas settled there, and it was in Darjeeling that Tenzing Norgay signed on to work for one of the first British Everest expeditions.

Sherpas joined many expeditions during the 1930s, travelling all over the Himalaya with the foreign mountaineers. Some of them, like Angtharkay and Pasang Dawa Lama, became very famous for their brilliant work.

After the Second World War foreigners were allowed into Nepal. For the first time Western mountaineers visited Sola Khumbu, the Sherpas' homeland, and Tenzing Norgay returned to his own land, to attempt the new southern route up Everest. Nowadays in virtually every Sherpa family one or more of its members works for expeditions and trekking parties. Sometimes they are better climbers than the foreign mountaineers who pay them – the Sherpas get the mountaineers up the mountain. All this work means that they have more money, but most Sherpa families keep up their small farms, and traditional way of life.

SKIING

Climbing mountains can seem a slow, boring business, which is why I sometimes enjoy the contrast of skiing. Skiing is about speed and excitement and the rush of air against your face, as you fly down the mountain. Skiing was only developed as a sport at the end of the nineteenth century, when an Englishman, Arnold Lunn, started to ski for fun in the Swiss Alps.

Skiing was invented by the Lapps, the nomadic people who live in the far north of Norway, Finland and Sweden. Their long wooden planks, curved up at the tips, were a means of travelling across deep snow without sinking, as they followed their herds of reindeer across the Arctic wilderness. Their boots were strapped to the skis with leather thongs, but only the toes were held down; their heels could lift up, so that they slid along with a running motion. It was with similar skis that Roald Amundsen and his companions crossed the wastes of Antarctica to reach the South Pole in 1912.

The early sport skiers used skis similar to those of the Lapps. To turn on steep slopes, they developed a technique called the Telemark, with one knee pushed forward and bent sharply, to curve the ski round.

Nowadays most people in Europe use modern 'alpine' skis with rigid bindings that clamp plastic boots into place, holding feet firmly on the skis, with heels down. The skis are made of metal, plastic and carbon, with razor sharp metal edges to grip the compacted snow of prepared runs. Top racers reach speeds of over

100 kph and their timings are measured in thousandths of a second. For most people, skiing is a gentler activity, taken at much slower speeds, but nearly everyone who tries it loves the thrill of gliding over the snow.

SKINS

Some skiers like to escape from the crowded ski lifts and prepared runs to travel across uninhabited mountains and many use Nordic skis. If you are doing this ski touring, you have to ski uphill as well as downhill. With some skis you can use special waxes to grip the snow, but the most reliable method, particularly on steep slopes, is to fix skins to the soles of your skis. Sealskin was originally used: the fur was placed with the hairs pointing down the hill. The ski could be slid forward but it would not slide backwards.

Nowadays skins are made from artificial nylon fur, which is better and lighter than sealskin. The fur is fixed to a tough strip of fabric the same length and width as your ski. Using a special glue you stick the skins onto your ski soles for climbing. When you reach your pass or summit and it is time to ski down the other side, you just peel off the skins and pack them away in your rucksack. No glue remains on the ski soles, and they are now free to glide smoothly on the downhill run.

SLEEPING BAGS see CLIMBING GEAR

SNOW

Eskimos have many different words for snow. Mountaineers and skiers also learn to recognize different types. It can be light and fluffy or as thick and heavy as porridge. Sometimes the surface melts and refreezes, forming a crust like an eggshell. For skiers the worst thing is a 'breakable crust', where one minute they are gliding on the surface and the next they are sinking into the powder beneath. Many skiers love new fluffy powder snow best of all. But for a climber, wading on foot, powder snow can be a nightmare. For climbers the perfect snow is 'névé', in which the snow has almost formed ice; it is hard and smooth, and crampons and ice axes bite into it firmly. What they hate most of all is 'sugar', great piles of unconsolidated crystals that offer no firm grip.

Snow is a very complicated substance. From the moment it falls out of the sky it is subjected to all kinds of pressure, from wind, sun, changing temperatures and its own weight as it piles up on the land. Although every snowflake starts life as a hexagonal crystal*, those crystals are constantly changing. Anyone who works or travels in the mountains needs to know something about those changes. Snow is beautiful and exciting, but it can also be extremely dangerous; it is important to know whether a particular slope is likely to avalanche. One method of judging a slope is to dig a 'profile'. Using an ice axe or shovel, you cut a trench through the snow so that you can examine the different layers and see how well they have stuck together.

SNOW BLINDNESS

Snow reflects light. It bounces the sun's rays into your eyes, so that even if you are staring at the ground your eyes can be strained. That is why you have to wear sun-glasses in the snow, particularly at high altitude, where the ultraviolet light is much more intense. Even in cloudy weather the ultraviolet can damage your eyes. If you ski or climb in snowy mountains without sun-glasses, you are likely to get headaches and bloodshot eyes. If you spend too long without protection you can become 'snow blind', which is much worse. For a day or two you can see nothing and every time you blink it feels as though sand is being rubbed across your eyeballs.

SNOWBRIDGE

When people walk on glaciers* they often have to cross natural bridges called snowbridges, which are formed by snow blowing across the tops of crevasses.* Sometimes the bridge is a single crossing point that is very clear to see, but often the whole length of a crevasse is hidden by a thin layer of snow just a few centimetres thick.

SNOW CAVE

The evening was drawing in and we knew that we would not reach the summit that day. Luke Hughes and I were at 7750 metres on the Tibetan peak of Shisha Pangma, isolated far above the rest of our team. It was late October and the temperature was about –30°C. We had no tent and no sleeping bags. But we had brought a lightweight snow shovel for emergencies.

At 4.00 p.m. we started digging into a bank of wind-firmed snow. At that altitude digging made us breathless and dizzy, so we took turns. Luckily there were no bands of hard ice to cut through and after about an hour we had a cave just big enough for the two of us.

We spent the next twelve hours in that cave, sitting on our climbing rope for insulation. We shivered but we were a lot warmer than we would have been outside. During the night a vicious wind blew up, blasting spindrift* across the mountain. Without our snow cave we would probably not have survived the night.

Snow caves have two advantages over tents. First, all you need to carry is a snow shovel and perhaps a snow saw. Second, unlike tents, they do not flap about in the wind. In 1990, during an expedition to the mountains of South Georgia,* in Antarctica, we made a luxurious snow cave for our base camp. We used a snow saw to cut blocks in the snow, which we levered out with a shovel.

After three days' work it was so big that we could pitch tents inside and walk around the two main rooms. Between the two rooms we had a fitted kitchen, with food shelves cut into the snow walls. For twenty-three days the cave provided secure shelter from raging blizzards.

To make a snow cave you first dig an entrance tunnel, just wide enough for one person to crawl through. Once the tunnel has penetrated about 2 metres into the slope, you start to enlarge the cave sideways, until there is enough room for everyone to sleep inside. Of course the further you dig from the entrance, the further you have to drag the snow blocks to throw them out. The best snow caves have raised platforms for sleeping, with a trench for the cold air to sink into.

You have to be careful to keep the walls of a snow cave thick enough. In Pakistan, we once dug a snow cave in too much of a hurry. The walls were so thin that they sagged during the night, pressing closer and closer down on our faces. That was one of the most unpleasant nights I have ever spent.

SNOW LEOPARD

Of all the wild animals in the mountains of Central Asia and the Himalaya,* the most rare and beautiful is the snow leopard. It is a little smaller than the common leopard, with thick smoky-grey fur, marked by black spots and rosettes, an unusually long thick tail for balance, and huge feet to prevent it sinking too deep into the snow. It roams high in the wilds, between 3000 and 6000 metres, though in winter it may shelter as low as 1000 metres in the protection of the forest. It has to cover huge distances, preying on isolated flocks of ibex and other wild goats and sheep. It also eats mice, hares and partridges and sometimes attacks domestic animals in the winter, when wild game is sparse.

Very little is known about the snow leopard because it has so rarely been seen by naturalists. Although snow leopards are now protected, some people still hunt them illegally, determined to get

their beautiful fur. Experts believe that there are only about 150 snow leopards left in Nepal and 250 in Pakistan. However, greater numbers are probably still roaming the immense open spaces to the north of the Himalaya.

SOLO

Lord Hunt, who led the first ascent of Everest in 1953, has often said that the rewarding thing about mountaineering is the friendship and comradeship that come from living together in the mountains. He is right, but mountaineering can also be a very personal, private experience. Some climbers like to be completely alone in the mountains. The satisfying thing about solo climbing is that you are totally responsible for yourself – your life is in your own hands. Some of the best mountaineers who have enjoyed solo climbing include Hermann Buhl,* Walter Bonatti,* and Catherine Destivelle.*

SOUTHERN ALPS OF NEW ZEALAND

Edmund Hillary was undoubtedly one of the strongest climbers on the 1953 Everest expedition: he had learned his mountaineering in the Southern Alps of New Zealand (Mount Cook, 3764 metres; Mount Aspiring, 3027 metres; and Mount Travers, 2338 metres). Although the summits of the Southern Alps are slightly lower than the European Alps, they are more serious. Storms sweep in frequently from the Tasman Sea. The glaciers* are huge and complicated, there are few paths and huts and many of the mountains are guarded by dense forest and bush. New Zealand climbers get used to long, hard treks carrying heavy rucksacks. They also gain experience on difficult snow and ice climbs. In 1953 the British Everest Expedition was very fortunate to have the help of two New Zealand climbers: George Lowe and his friend, Ed Hillary.

SOUTH GEORGIA

Ernest Shackleton was not a mountaineer. He was a sailor and polar explorer, but in 1916 he achieved a great feat of mountaineering after his ship, HMS *Endurance*, sank off Antarctica. He and his crew escaped to the tiny uninhabited Elephant Island, hundreds of kilometres away from any help. In a desperate bid to seek rescue, Shackleton sailed, with five companions in one of the remaining lifeboats, the 1150 miles to the island of South Georgia.

At that time there were whaling stations on the east coast of South Georgia from which people could organize a rescue. But Shackleton's tiny boat was washed up on the west coast. Between Shackleton and help lay a great range of mountains and glaciers,* unknown, unmapped. The only climbing equipment for the men was a short length of hemp rope, a carpenter's adze and some nails from the boat hammered into their boot soles to grip the ice.

Ernest Shackleton

Storms sweep almost constantly across the mountains of South Georgia. There are occasional fine spells but, once he started the crossing, Shackleton dared not stop in case he was caught in a blizzard. He was also worried that if the exhausted men went to sleep they would never wake up. They kept moving, through night and day, for thirty-six hours, finding their way round huge crevasses,* crossing ridges, sliding down steep gullies* and finally roping down a great waterfall that blocked their way. No one knew where they were. One mistake and the men waiting on Elephant Island would never be rescued. But Shackleton and his companions succeeded in crossing the mountains to the whaling station, where the manager was astonished to see them.

Several weeks later the twenty-eight men on Elephant Island, by now almost starving, were rescued, thanks to the determination of Ernest Shackleton, the sailor who had briefly become a mountaineer.

SPINDRIFT

It gets in your eyes. It pours down the back of your neck. It comes rushing down with a whistling, whispering sound, smothering you in icy powder. Wind causes spindrift, whipping up fine powder snow and pouring it down mountain gullies* to make life a nightmare for any climber caught underneath.

STOVES see CLIMBING GEAR

SUMMITS

Most people who climb mountains do it because they enjoy the climbing for its own sake. However, the ultimate aim is usually to reach a summit, the highest point of the mountain. Sometimes it is rocky; often it is overlaid with snow. The summit of Everest,* for instance, is a flattish mound of snow about the size of a large table. Some summits consist of an overhanging cornice* of snow, so dangerous that no one dares to stand on the highest point. On Kangchenjunga, the world's third highest peak, mountaineers stop a few metres below the top because it is a holy mountain and they do not want to offend the local people.

The summit of Cerro Torre, in Patagonia, is a gigantic mushroom of snow and ice, perched 30 metres above the top of the rock tower. Some climbers say that because the mushroom is made of frozen water it is not permanent and therefore not part of the mountain; they stop at the top of the rock.

One of the most exciting summits in the world is the tip of the Aiguille de la République, in the French Alps. It is a slender needle of smooth, holdless granite. The usual way to climb the last few metres is to lasso the summit with a rope, pull up and cling to the sharp point. Only a trapeze artist would be able actually to stand on the summit.

Many mountains have several summits. Often, on the first ascent of a mountain, it is not clear until the last minute exactly which is the highest point. Once you really do reach the summit, it is always an emotional moment. The emotions are very mixed: relief, perhaps, at not having to climb any further; deep satisfaction at completing a project after maybe several weeks' work; joy at just being there, up in the sky; gratitude, on a first ascent, for the chance to be where no one has ever been before; worry, sometimes, that now the hardest part – the descent – is about to begin.

TABLE MOUNTAIN

One of the best day's climbing I ever had was on the edge of a huge city. We drove out of town at dawn and half an hour later we were climbing up vertical cliffs to the summit of a famous mountain. The city lay spread beneath us and beyond it was the ocean.

The city is one of the world's great sea ports, Cape Town, at the southern tip of South Africa. The mountain is Table Mountain, a giant, flat-topped block of sandstone. Rock climbers love the spectacular walls of Table Mountain. Most of the climbs are vertical or overhanging, but the Cape sandstone has many horizontal cracks, giving huge hand and footholds, like rungs on a ladder.

Table Mountain is also famous for its many hundreds of plant species, growing in the ravines and on the great plateau of its summit. The vegetation of South Africa's Cape Province is unique and is called 'fynbos'. The best known fynbos plants are of the beautiful protea species. A protea flower is the national emblem of South Africa. There are 2,500 species of plant on Table Mountain alone – more than there are in the whole of the British Isles!

TENTS see **CLIMBING GEAR**

TENZING

Sherpa Tenzing was born in sight of Everest.* When he was a boy he often gazed up at the mountain, while he was out on the high pastures, looking after his parents'

yaks.* In the 1930s he went to live in Darjeeling, to look for work with the foreign expeditions* that came to attempt Kangchenjunga, Everest and other peaks. Over the years he climbed all over the Himalaya with British, French and Swiss expeditions. Unlike most of his Sherpa* friends he did not think of expeditions just as a job of work. He had his own climbing ambitions and he wanted desperately to climb Everest.

Tenzing's life seemed to be going well and he became known as Tenzing Norgay, the Fortunate One. Then in 1952 he had his first big chance when his Swiss friends asked him to be *sirdar* (head Sherpa) for their attempt on Everest. Tenzing climbed within about 200 metres of the summit, higher than anyone had been before. In the autumn the Swiss made another attempt. Tenzing joined them once more, but they were again unsuccessful. Tenzing returned, exhausted, to his family in Darjeeling. A few months later the British arrived in Nepal. Once again Tenzing Norgay was employed both as *sirdar* and as a full member of the climbing team. This time he achieved his most precious dream: on 29 May 1953, he stood with Edmund Hillary* on the highest spot on Earth.

After his success on Everest, Tenzing Norgay became world famous. He also became much richer: he was able to send three of his children to university in America. Although the mountains had given him much pleasure, he wanted to be sure that they would never have to carry loads up dangerous slopes to earn a living.

TERRACES

Mountain farmers have to create fields on impossibly steep slopes, so they terrace the slopes, cutting out a series of horizontal steps where earth and crops will not slide away. Each field may be only a few metres wide, supported by a stone wall. It is impossible to use tractors on these tiny shelves so all the work has to be done by human or animal labour.

The Incas* built terraces on the Andean slopes of Peru. All over the Asian mountains people also created terraces, to grow rice, wheat, barley and potatoes, often mingled with fruit and nut trees. Terraces are a beautiful sight, rising like giant green staircases up the mountains. However, in some areas like Nepal the population is increasing so fast that more and more mountain slopes are being terraced, eating away at vital forests.

THIN AIR

As you climb higher, the air pressure decreases, and the level of oxygen and other gases falls proportionately. This means that you have to take several lungfuls of air in order to get the same amount of oxygen that one lungful might have given you at a lower altitude. To counteract this, mountaineers often carry bottled oxygen on the very highest peaks, in strong metal pressurized cylinders. On top of the cylinder is a regulator valve which lets the oxygen escape into a rubber tube. This tube leads to a mask, allowing the climber to breath in the oxygen. To have any useful effect, the climber needs to be breathing in three or four litres a minute.

Bottled oxygen was used to make the first ascents of the world's five highest peaks. It certainly makes climbing easier and safer at those extreme altitudes, but the problems are weight and cold: someone has to carry all those cylinders, and because the air outside is so cold, a climber's breath tends to freeze inside the mask and tubes. The ice eventually blocks the oxygen supply, and it isn't always easy to stop and clear it! (See also ALTITUDE SICKNESS.)

TIBET

For centuries it was a forbidden land, hidden behind the great wall of the Himalaya.* The few travellers who managed to enter Tibet, brought back tales of a harsh land, a high treeless desert, swept by biting cold winds, ringed by huge mountains and sparsely populated by tough nomads. But they also told of the magnificent Potala palace at Lhasa, home of the Dalai Lama, Tibet's Buddhist ruler.

Tibet is indeed a harsh land but there is something beautiful about that immense open space, the highest country in the world. It is a huge country: if you place the map of Tibet diagonally across the map of Europe, it stretches lengthwise from the Pyrenees to Warsaw; widthwise from Italy to Rotterdam.

Many Tibetans are still nomads, roaming the land with their sheep and yaks.* The Potala palace still towers over Lhasa, but most of the Buddhist monasteries have disappeared.

Foreigners have always tried to control Tibet because it commands such a huge area right at the heart of Central Asia. During the nineteenth century, the British government of India was worried that the Russians might take over Tibet. Eventually, in 1904, a British army invaded the country and forced the Dalai Lama into a trade agreement with British India. However, Tibet remained independent. Then, in 1950, China invaded, forcing Communism on the Tibetans, imprisoning anyone who argued and destroying 90 per cent of the country's Buddhist monasteries. Ever since then the Dalai Lama has lived in exile in India.

A few years ago the Chinese government started to allow foreigners into Tibet again. For mountaineers it was a chance to attempt the north side of the great Himalayan peaks like Everest.*

Most of Tibet is very dry, but in the south-east, on the borders of Bhutan, Assam, Burma and Szechuan, the land is affected by the wet weather of the monsoon. It is an area of dense forest, cut by huge river gorges. This eastern part of the Himalaya* is still barely explored and there are hundreds of unclimbed mountains.

TREASURY OF THE FIVE SNOWS

The air is filled with a murmur of Indian women's voices. They move in their bright-coloured saris among the bushes, picking the young leaf tips and putting them into baskets on their backs. The terraced hillside is covered by a green carpet of smooth-cropped bushes: the famous tea gardens of Darjeeling. Behind the tea pickers, about 60 kilometres away, a great shimmering curtain seems to hang in the sky, the snows of the Himalaya.* One massive peak with five summits dominates everything. It is Kangchenjunga, the Treasury of the Five Snows.

Kangchenjunga is a holy mountain, revered by the people of Sikkim, the mountain state just north of Darjeeling. For this reason the Maharaja of Sikkim was never keen on foreign climbers attempting the mountain, the third highest in the world. When it was finally climbed in 1955 the expedition leader, Charles Evans, promised the Maharaja that no one would touch the summit.

The expedition found a route from the Nepalese side, up the south-west face of the mountain to the main summit (8595 metres). The first two to reach the summit were George Band and Joe Brown, who was then probably the best rock climber in the world. The final obstacle was a difficult vertical crack in the rock cliff. On his home cliffs near Manchester, Joe Brown would have climbed it easily. Here, about 8500 metres above sea level, he needed a little help. He turned his oxygen set up to the maximum rate of 6 litres (see THIN AIR), got up the crack, then brought up Band on the rope.

A few more steps and they could see the summit in front of them. But they kept the leader's promise and stopped just a few metres below the final mound of snow.

TROLL WALL

The highest pure rock wall in Europe is Norway's Troll Wall: the North Face of Trollryggen, which is plumb vertical for over 1200 metres. It was first climbed by a British team in 1965. They had to make five bivouacs* on the climb. Twenty-two years later, in 1989, another British climber, Phil Thornhill, or Fearless Phil as the press called him later, came to climb the wall alone, in the middle of winter.

Thornhill knew that the climb would take a long time and took with him a gigantic haul sack full of food and gear. Before setting off he left a note on his car windscreen, saying that he would be back in about a month.

He climbed slowly, using a rope to protect himself and another to haul up the sack full of supplies. After each pitch or rope-length, he had to abseil* down, then climb back up the rope, removing all the pitons, nuts and friends that he had placed on that pitch for protection. So, like the famous solo climber Walter Bonatti* Thornhill climbed each section twice. To make life even more difficult, it was winter, the temperature was below freezing and snow and ice were clinging to the cliff.

Thornhill crept slowly up the wall. After spending four weeks completely alone he was getting close to the top. Then on the twenty-eighth day a piton came out. Thornhill only fell about ten metres before the rope held him on another anchor, but as he swung into the rock there was a ghastly cracking noise. His right leg was broken above the knee.

It was a nightmare – a lone climber, stuck 1000 metres up Europe's biggest precipice, in the middle of winter, with an agonizing injury. He had a desperate struggle to haul himself into his little bivouac tent, perched on a ledge. Later that day he started to shout, hoping that someone in the valley would hear. Luckily they did. They also read the note on the car and realized who was stuck up on the Troll Wall.

Four days later a helicopter* flew past with a big banner saying, 'Wait there, Mr Thornhill. We are coming to get you.' Eventually the rescue team lowered climbers on cables from the summit and Phil Thornhill was winched to safety, and whisked off to hospital. Although the accident had stopped him completing his amazing climb, Thornhill had probably established a new record: he had spent thirty-two days completely alone on a mountain wall.

Trollryggen is just one of Norway's many mountains, which stretch right up into the Arctic. Most Norwegians enjoy the outdoors and nearly everyone climbs and treks in the mountains. In the winter people go on long ski treks, using lightweight Nordic or *langlauf* skis to glide through the forests and across the high plateaux, staying each night at mountain huts.

TSAMPA

When Tibetans make a long journey through the mountains they take a special high-altitude ration called *tsampa*. It is made from barley flour, precooked and ground into a fine powder. They eat it plain or mix it in hot tea, with butter and salt to make a kind of soup. This tea takes some getting used to, but when you are tired and hungry and there is nothing else to eat, it can taste quite good. It is also very nutritious, with a lot of energy-giving fat.

TSANGPO

One of the curious things about the Himalaya* is that although many of its rivers rise on the north side of the range they nearly all flow eventually south into the Indian Ocean. The Indus flows hundreds of miles north-west before plunging down through

Pakistan to the sea port of Karachi. The Tsangpo rises very close to the Indus source, near the holy Mount Kailas in Tibet, but it flows in completely the opposite direction – eastward along the northern side of the Himalaya – before carving its way down in a great bend to the plains of Assam and Bangladesh, where it is called the Brahmaputra.

For a long time geographers were not sure whether the Tsangpo river in Tibet was the same river as the Brahmaputra that flowed down on the south side of the Himalaya. In 1880 Kintup, one of the Pundits* – the secret surveyors trained by the British Survey of India – was sent to try to solve the riddle of the Tsangpo. Kintup was away for several years. At one point he was imprisoned by the authorities in Tibet, but he managed to escape and find his way into the far eastern corner of the country, where the Tsangpo plunges down into a great gorge, hemmed in by forest-cloaked walls. His instructions were to throw five specially marked logs into the river each day for ten days. Observers would be waiting hundreds of miles away, down on the banks of the Brahmaputra, to see whether the logs arrived. Sadly, many months had now passed since Kintup set off on his journey. Although he dutifully carried out his task, no one was watching the river on the south side of the Himalaya. However, Kintup saw enough of the general lie of the land to be fairly sure that this Tsangpo must be the same river as the Brahmaputra.

Many years later British explorers were allowed into eastern Tibet and confirmed that Kintup had been correct. They named one of the great rapids, where the Tsangpo starts its headlong plunge through the Himalaya, Kintup's Falls.

TUNNELS

Mountains are always a problem for road and railway builders. Sometimes the easiest but most expensive answer is to build a tunnel through the mountains. When the Russians invaded Afghanistan in 1979, they were helped by the Salang tunnel, a road tunnel through the Hindu Kush mountains. In Europe, engineers started tunnelling railways under the Alps back in the nineteenth century. Now there are also road tunnels, like the famous 12-kilometre Mont Blanc tunnel. Although it is not exactly beneath Mont Blanc*, it does pass underneath the nearby summit of the Aiguille de Midi. At that point there are 2550 metres of solid granite above the roof of the tunnel.

The Mont Blanc tunnel has improved road connections between France and Italy. However, the beautiful Aosta valley on the Italian side, which used to be a peaceful dead-end, is now filled with the roar and smell of motor traffic.

URALS

Europe and Asia are really one large continent. However, we usually describe them as separate continents. The dividing line is the long chain of the Ural mountains, which splits Russia in two. The Urals are not huge mountains (the highest is 1640 metres), but they stretch 2500 kilometres from the Arctic ocean in the north, nearly to the Aral sea in the south.

VINSON

Antarctica is so vast that no one knew about the Sentinel range until 1935 when the Americans Lincoln Ellsworth and Herbert Hollick-Kenyon flew over it. Later it was discovered that one of these mountains, Mount Vinson, was the highest in Antarctica. It was first climbed by an American expedition during the Antarctic summer of 1966–7. Nowadays it is climbed several times each year, but it is a very expensive adventure. First you have to fly to Chile, then pay over £10,000 for a special flight to the remote Antarctic ice cap. Strangely, many people spend this huge sum to come and climb Vinson, yet all over the Antarctic continent there are hundreds of magnificent, unknown, unclimbed mountains.

VOLCANOES

In 1982 a massive explosion in Mexico filled the surrounding air for hundreds of miles with clouds of ash. The top had blown off a mountain called El Chichon. Like many mountains around the world, El Chichon is a volcano. It was created by lava – molten rock – blasting out through a weak area in the earth's surface to form a great cone of debris. Most volcanoes are cone-shaped, like Japan's Mount Fuji, and Mount Egmont of North Island, New Zealand. Even if they are not perfect cones, volcanic mountains are nearly always isolated, rounded humps. Kilimanjaro in Africa, Cotopaxi in Ecuador and Rainier in North America are all giants that stand alone.

Most volcanoes have a summit crater, the hollow out of which the molten rock used to spew. Sometimes it is still smoking and sending up occasional rocks, ashes and gases. Salcantay, in South America, is still active. Mount St Helen's, in North America, was thought to be extinct until a few years ago when a vast chunk of the mountain suddenly exploded into the air, showering hundreds of square kilometres with burning rock.

France has ancient extinct volcanoes in the Massif Central. However, further south in Europe there are active volcanoes: Mount Etna, on the island of Sicily, still erupts regularly, ejecting molten rock over the fields below. Most famous of the Italian volcanoes is Vesuvius, which last erupted in 1944. In AD 79 there was a massive eruption on Vesuvius, which destroyed the Roman city Pompeii.

LUCY WALKER

The first women climbers in the nineteenth century used to set off in long skirts. In those days it was unthinkable for 'ladies' to appear in public wearing trousers, and it was only after they passed the last houses that the women would slip off their skirts, to reveal climbing breeches underneath. However, one woman climber, Lucy Walker, always wore pale print dresses over her climbing boots, even on the mountain. In 1871, in her long dress, she made the first female ascent of the Matterhorn.*

WARFARE

Mountains often form frontiers, which invading armies have to cross. Both Hannibal the Great and Napoleon had to lead their armies over high Alpine passes to invade Italy. During the First World War Austrian and Italian troops spent four years fighting over the limestone peaks of the Dolomites.* Soldiers were stationed in caves and dug-outs, guarding high summits, where the winter temperature drops to –30°C.

During the Second World War Yugoslav resistance fighters operated in the Julian Alps, where it was hard for the German invaders to get at them. Many of them died and today you can visit their memorial sculpture, just below the summit of the highest mountain in Slovenia (the former Yugoslavia), Triglav. The memorial is a giant steel piton, 5 metres high, with a huge karabiner hanging from its eye.

The most recent mountain war is still being fought in the disputed state of Kashmir. The northern part of Kashmir is a mountain wilderness, but each side wants to control the area. For several years Indian and Pakistani troops have been stationed on high passes* in the Karakoram, fighting over the Siachen glacier, one of the largest glaciers* in Asia. Occasionally a soldier is killed by bullets, but the principal dangers are from avalanches,* crevasses,* cold and altitude sickness.*

WATER

For millions of people mountains are a vital source of water. When clouds drift against mountains, the water vapour is released as rain or snow, which eventually finds its way down to the valleys. Most of the world's great rivers start either as mountain streams or as murky torrents pouring out of glacier* tongues. Mountain lakes are frequently used as reservoirs, for storing drinking water, or to supply hydro-electric generators.

Hydro-electricity works on a simple principle. Water falls at high speed, channelled into turbines, which are like giant propellors. The water drives the turbines round in a magnetic field and this produces an electric current. Switzerland's mountains are full of dams, tunnels and special pipes, making the most of what the mountains have to offer – gravity. The great advantages of hydro-electricity are (a) that it is sustainable and that (b) it does not pollute. However, it is sad to see great metal pipes and concrete structures littering the mountains, and valleys flooded by new dams.

WHITEOUT

In a blizzard everything turns white. All horizons and shapes disappear. Snow and sky merge into a uniform whiteness. Mountain whiteouts can be terrifying, whether you are on the Cairngorm plateau in Scotland or on the summit of Everest.* All the shapes you normally recognize – ripples in the snow, the dip of a crevasse,* or the dangerous bulge of a cornice* – disappear. Without realizing it you can start walking round in circles. It was in whiteout conditions that the famous Austrian mountaineer, Hermann Buhl, wandered too close to the edge of a huge cornice. One minute he was on the ridge; the next he had vanished with a great bang as the cornice snapped.

Moving in a whiteout is always difficult, especially if you are on skis. Your sense of balance goes and you cannot tell whether you are going up or down. If you are caught by whiteout conditions on a mountain, you need to know how to use a map and compass and if there is the slightest risk of falling over a drop or into a crevasse, you need to be roped to your companions.

WIND

The fastest wind speed ever recorded was 231 mph – three times hurricane force. It was recorded at 1.21 p.m. on 12 April 1934 at the observatory on the summit of Mount Washington, 2000 metres above sea level. Mount Washington rises considerably higher than any of its neighbours in the Presidential range in North America, so it is like an island in a stream, alone against the raging currents of the air.

Mount Washington is notorious for its bad weather, but all around the world mountains tend to cause high winds. Wind helped to shape the mountains and is one of the main things that affects snow conditions.

High in the earth's atmosphere is a violent wind called the jet stream. In winter the jet stream often drops to below 8000 metres, which is why the highest Himalayan peaks are so difficult to climb in winter. During winter the upper slopes of Everest* are usually blasted clear of snow, leaving bare ice and rock.

XIXABANGMA

It is always hard to find words beginning with X. However, when the Chinese occupied Tibet* they gave Chinese spellings to all the place names: Shegar, a famous old mountain fortress, became Xegar; Shisha Pangma became Xixabangma.

Xixabangma is the only one of the fourteen peaks over 8000 metres that lies completely within Tibet, not touching a frontier. It was first climbed by a Chinese expedition in 1964. Now that foreigners are allowed into Tibet, it is climbed quite often by Western expeditions.

YAK

In the far north of Tibet,* on the bleak windswept plains of the Chang Tang, between 5000 and 6000 metres above sea level, there still roam herds of wild yaks, but nearly all Asia's yaks are now domesticated.

The yak is a cow adapted for life at high altitude. Its barrel chest houses huge lungs that can cope with the thin air* up to 6000 metres above sea level. Its legs are short and sturdy for climbing steep slopes. It has elegant spreading horns, soft dark eyes and a long hairy tail. Its body is also covered in long thick hair, which hangs to the ground in winter, like a great shaggy curtain, protecting the animal from biting winds, and forming a mattress when it lies on the hard frozen ground.

You can see yaks in the Himalayan regions of Pakistan, India, Nepal and Bhutan, but Tibet is the real home of the yak. It cannot live comfortably below about 4000 metres and it is happiest on the open slopes above the tree line. For a Tibetan or Sherpa* family their yaks are their most precious possessions. They provide milk, butter, cheese and a strong wool. They work as pack animals, carrying huge loads strapped to their backs. Their dung provides fertilizer or, if wood is scarce, it is dried and used to fuel the kitchen stove. Once a year the butcher is called to slaughter one or two of the older beasts, which then provide meat and leather for the family.

Male yaks are usually dark brown; females jet black. However there are many variations and yaks are frequently crossed with domestic cows to produce 'dzos'. Whether dzos or yaks, they are always a charming sight on the upper valleys and trade routes of the Himalaya* and the mountains often echo with the sound of their jangling cowbells.

YETI

In Kathmandu, capital of the Himalayan kingdom of Nepal, there is a well-known restaurant called the Yak and Yeti. The yak is a familiar animal in the Himalaya,* but the yeti . . . well, no one knows for certain whether it actually exists.

Yeti is a Sherpa* word from *yeh* (rocky place) and *teh* (that type of animal), so it is an animal that lives in rocky places. According to the Sherpas there are two types of yeti, both ape-like creatures which walk upright and are covered in reddish brown hair. The smaller type is quite common and eats small mammals. The larger, rarer type stands $2^1/_2$ metres tall, will kill cattle or yaks and has occasionally eaten humans.

The Sherpas are not the only people to talk about yetis. As far away as the Pamirs, Mongolia and the Caucasus, Russians have reported seeing unknown apemen and finding mysterious tracks in the snow. In Nepal several famous Western mountaineers have reported unusual tracks. The British mountaineer Don Whillans, renowned for his toughness, was very frightened one night at Annapurna base camp, when he looked out of his tent to see a large creature running across the snow. In 1952 Eric Shipton photographed a large footprint in the snow, showing distinct toes. The line of tracks led for hundreds of metres across the glacier* and had been made by a creature walking upright.

Despite all these rumours and reports, no one has ever managed to photograph a yeti. Edmund Hillary* says that many of the reported footprints are just the tracks of common mountain animals like wild goats, enlarged by the effect of the sun melting the snow. However, that does not explain the fresh tracks with clear indentations. They could have been made by bears, which are common

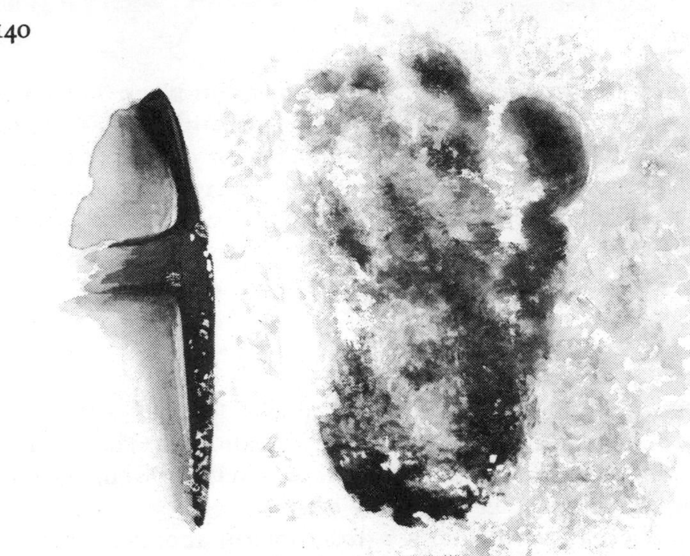

in the Himalaya, but bears would leave claw marks and rarely walk upright for more than a few metres. Another possibility is that they are the tracks of barefoot humans. Sherpas and other Himalayan people sometimes walk barefoot in the snow and tend to have very wide feet. However, the toes in Shipton's photo look very odd for a human!

So far there is no satisfactory explanation but if yetis do exist, they do not live on the glaciers;* the tracks are made when they cross from one valley to another. Their home must be deep in the densely forested gorges that surround the mountains of Nepal and eastern Tibet.* There are still many valleys where humans have hardly penetrated and it is just possible that an unknown apeman lives hidden there.

YODELLING

Every mountain area has its traditional music. In the Andes* it is the banjos and breathy pan-pipes of the South American Indians, in the Caucasus, the balalaika. The eastern Himalaya* echoes with the drums, cymbals and horns of Buddhist monks, and long horns similar to the European alpenhorn.* The Alps* are also famous for Austrian and Swiss folk songs full of yodelling, a strange high-pitched noise, half-way between singing and croaking. The musicians dance and yodel, accompanied by harmoniums. The men wear traditional *lederhosen* – leather shorts – and the women wear intricately embroidered bodices with full dirndl skirts.

YUKON

In the far north of Canada, on the border with Alaska, there is a province called Yukon Territory, where at the end of the nineteenth century, in remote outposts like Klondike, people came rushing to search for gold. Yukon is a land of mountains and the biggest mountains are near the Pacific coast.

Captain Cook, the great sailor-explorer, first noticed these mountains during one of his voyages and named the most prominent peak Mount St Elias, because it was seen on St Elias's Day. In 1897 an Italian explorer, the Duke of Abruzzi, landed on the icy shore and used a team of dog sledges to travel inland, crossing glaciers* to reach and climb the mighty peak. Later an even bigger peak, hidden further inland was discovered: Mount Logan.

Mount Logan is colossal. In sheer bulk it is probably the biggest mountain in the world. The highest point is 5951 metres above sea level – not very high compared to the Himalayan* giants, but Logan's walls rise straight up, 4250 metres from the surrounding glaciers, and the summit plateau stretches for 17 kilometres, like a gigantic, icy version of South Africa's Table Mountain.*

Each summer a handful of people come to attempt Mount Logan and other peaks in this wild corner of Yukon. They fly from the nearest airstrip, 200 kilometres away. The aircraft lands on skis, dumps the climbers then flies off, leaving them alone at the heart of an immense ice wilderness. Climbing and skiing in this part of Yukon is a real adventure, requiring skill, experience and careful planning. Reaching the summits also requires some luck, for storms frequently sweep in from the nearby Pacific Ocean.

YURT

The yurt is the finest tent in the world. For many of the nomadic people of Central Asia who move around the Pamirs, the Tien Shan and the Altai mountains, yurts are their only homes.

The yurt is extremely heavy, and has to be carried on the backs of yaks* or camels. Usually a whole family lives in a yurt and it may stay pitched in the same place for months on end. It is circular with a slightly domed roof. The walls are made from a wooden lattice framework which supports the wooden roof struts. Rush matting is wrapped round the frame for insulation then the whole yurt is covered in sheets of thick felted wool, which keep out wind, rain and snow. Inside the floor is carpeted and the walls are hung with rich colourful rugs and tapestries. The centre of the yurt is dominated by an iron stove with a chimney disappearing up through a flap in the roof. Around the edge of the central room curtains provide some privacy for little bedrooms.

ZANSKAR

Zanskar is like a hidden mountain kingdom. Whichever direction you come from you have to cross several high mountain passes* in order to reach the province. To the south and west lie ridge after ridge of Himalayan peaks. To the north the Earth's crust is crumpled up into the great ranges of Ladakh and the Karakoram. To the east lies the vast plateau of Tibet.* There are still only two roads into Zanskar and they can only be used by heavy trucks.

Although Zanskar lies within the modern frontiers of India, it has more in common with Tibet. The people are Tibetan and their religion is Tibetan Buddhism. Since the 1950s, when China destroyed most of Tibet's monasteries, Zanskar has been the richest centre for Tibetan culture.

ZERMATT

Without the Matterhorn,* Zermatt would be an unknown little village, but ever since Edward Whymper and his companions made the first ascent of the mountain from this valley in 1865, Zermatt has been one of the world's most famous holiday resorts. One family in particular, the Seilers, was responsible for developing Zermatt, building some of the best hotels in Switzerland. By the beginning of the twentieth century skiing was becoming a popular sport. Now Zermatt has some of the longest mountain railways* and cable cars in the world. The ski runs are very good, although not the best in the Alps.* However, that does not matter. For each person who comes to Zermatt, to walk, climb, ski, or just to relax in an hotel, there is an unforgettable moment when they come round a corner and there, seeming to hang in the sky far above the valley, is the unmistakable outline of one of the world's most famous mountains: the Matterhorn.

INDEX